A FRESH START

by

John Chapman

HODDER & STOUGHTON
LONDON SYDNEY AUCKLAND TORONTO

Acknowledgments

All Scripture quotations, unless otherwise indicated, are from the New International Version of the Bible, copyrighted 1978 by New York International Bible Society. Published in Great Britain and Australia by Hodder & Stoughton Ltd. Used by permission.

P.52. Lines quoted from There is a Green Hill Far Away. C. F. Alexander (1818–1895).

British Library Cataloguing in Publication Data

Chapman, John C.
   A fresh start.———(Hodder Christian paperbacks)
   1. Converts
   I. Title
   248.'46   BV4916

   ISBN 0–340–34330–3

Contents

1. Where is it With You?

Part 1 — Our Problem, God's Solution

2. Sometimes I'm Treated Like a Block of Wood   15
3. Something is Terribly Wrong   22
4. What has God Done About it?   38
5. What's it Like to be a Christian?   64

Part 2 — Can We Really Know?

6. Will the True God Please Stand up?   83
7. Impressive, Outrageous, but Believable   87
8. The Lord in His World   106
9. Can I Trust the Gospels?   116

Part 3 — What's the alternative?

10. What's the Hurry?   131
11. Why Isn't Good Enough, Good Enough?   141

Part 4 — What's to be done?

12. What am I Supposed to do?   149
13. Can I be Sure?   163
14. Which Way is Forward?   177

P.S. . .   194

To Paul, Jim and Hazel

Foreword

Christian Beliefs is a series intended to communicate various aspects of the theory and practice of the Christian faith.

The contributing authors are Australian, for we believe that God is blessing His people in our land by raising up Christian leaders who have the ability to communicate their positive Christian beliefs. Their ministries are varied, and encompass a wide range of speaking, teaching and preaching situations throughout Australia and increasingly, overseas. The publication of these books will extend these ministries of proclaiming the Word of God, even further.

With the publishers, I am committed as General Editor, to producing a series which is firmly based upon God's Word—the Bible.

A Fresh Start. . . by John C. Chapman, Th.L. (Hons.)

In *Know and Tell the Gospel*, John Chapman gave us an effective *how to do it* book about spreading the Christian message.

But what is the Christian message, and how does one receive it?

In this volume, a *what is it* book, the Author explains the message of the gospel of Jesus Christ, and sets out the first steps a person must take to become a believing, committed Christian.

John Chapman's gift of simple explanation and his famous sense of humour make this a very readable book. If you have been searching for a book which explains, either for your own or another's benefit, what is involved in becoming a Christian, your search may now be over.

PAUL BARNETT
Series Editor.

Robert Menzies College
Macquarie University
New South Wales
Australia   May 1983

Preface

You may have been given this book by a friend or you may have just picked it up. It deals with how we can become friends with the living God.

It is written for people who are prepared to look into Christianity. It sets out the fundamentals. My hope is that it will help you in your pilgrimage back to God.

I have been a Christian for more than thirty years. I find each year more exciting than the one before. I still cannot get over the fact that God should care so much for me that He sent His Son into the world so that I could become friends with Him. That friendship has been so satisfying to me over the years that I want everyone to share it with me.

I hope the book helps.

I have quoted freely from the Bible. You may be unfamiliar with it. It might help you if I point out that a reference such as (Luke 2:10) means that the quotation comes from a book in the Bible called "The Gospel according to Saint Luke". "Luke" is in the New Testament, 2 is the chapter number and 10 is the paragraph number in chapter 2 of Luke's Gospel.

My thanks go to Paul Barnett who encouraged me to write this book; to Phillip Jensen and Junee and Royle Hawkes who read it and made valuable suggestions; and Janet Kearsley who typed it.

John Chapman
May 1983

CHAPTER ONE

Where is it With You?

I remember hearing a story about a small child who asked, "Dad, where did I come from?" The slightly embarrassed father sat his child down and went through a long involved explanation about the birds and the bees and the flowers. The child showed a degree of surprise and interest. When the father had finished, he asked "Is that clear?" His son replied, "Yes, quite clear and very interesting, but all I wanted to know was where I came from. Tommy Jones says that he came from England and I want to know where I came from?"

Over the last ten years I have spoken to hundreds of people about becoming Christians. Some of them believed in God, some of them were uncertain even about His existence. Some who believed in God were not sure whether Jesus Christ was God's Son, while others already believed this. Some believed Jesus to be the Son of God but just did not want to change their way of life, while others did want to become Christians but did not know what to do.

None of us is at exactly the same place in our spiritual life, and this presents me with a slight problem. I do not want to bore you with answers to questions which you are not asking. Yet I want to cover the ground so that a proper investigation of Christianity can be made, therefore I have written this book in four parts.

Part 1 deals with God's solution to our problem. It assumes the existence of God, that Jesus Christ is God's unique Son, and that the Bible gives accurate information about God.

Part 2 is written for those who are uncertain about God's existence and whether Jesus was God's Son. It also sets out to show that the New Testament histories about Jesus are reliable and that the Bible does give us accurate information about God. If these are not your questions you may like to skip this section and proceed to Part 3 or Part 4.

Part 3 deals with the serious responsibility of responding to God in His way rather than our own.

Part 4 sets out in detail, what we need to do to become Christians, and how we can be sure we are Christians.

Part 1

Our Problem, God's Solution

CHAPTER TWO

Sometimes I'm Treated Like a Block of Wood

My normal pattern in the morning is to set the alarm for 6 am, turn on the radio news and listen to what has been happening in the rest of the world while I've been sleeping in my part of it. Then I work out if it's worth getting out of bed. Up till now it's been O.K.

One morning I heard of the assassination of President Sadat of Egypt. To my knowledge no one has ever tried to murder me, but as I thought over that morning's news, I was convinced again that the act of assassination demonstrates the ultimate in a broken relationship. Not only does the assassin not want to be a friend with his victim but his action is deliberately designed to ensure the impossibility of friendship developing in the future. He removes the other person from the scene. It is a fairly ruthless denial of relationship. It says in quite an unmistakable way, "I don't want you as a friend."

I just ignore Him
There are other ways of rejecting people which demonstrate the same idea but are not so dramatic in application. Once at a meeting I made what I thought was a helpful and very valuable contribution. Deathly silence followed, and after a convenient pause, the discussion continued as if I had not spoken at all. My contribution was ignored. That was bad enough, but even worse was the realisation that I had been rejected. I had been treated as if I were a block of wood, and what is more, I knew

it. I have experienced the same feeling of rejection when someone comes into a room and relates to everyone else, but not to me. Sometimes this may be unintentional carelessness, but when it is deliberate, the rejection is as clear as if I had been given the 'Sadat' treatment. Such rejection is always hurtful and usually makes me angry. "I'm here," I want to cry out. "I mightn't be too bright but I am a person. I'm not a nothing, and I'm certainly more significant than a lump of wood."

Whenever it happens I censure such behaviour. Yet we are strange people. Why do I censure behaviour in others which I excuse or even encourage in myself? Although I hate it when I am ignored, I once had no difficulty relating to God in exactly that way. I just ignored Him. I didn't want to worry Him and I didn't want Him to worry me. I lived in a world which told me He was there. I wasn't unaware of His existence, nor did I doubt it. Yet I related to Him as if He were a block of wood. The rejection was as plain as if I had gone on an anti-christian rampage. Could I expect God to be anything but hurt by my reaction to Him? I had passed judgment on myself by my own angry attitude towards those who by ignoring me, had rejected me.

Always when I'm in trouble

One night I gave a lift in my car to a young man who was hitch-hiking.

"What sort of a night have you had?" I asked.

"So, so! I've been to see my girl friend. Yours?"

"Good."

"What do you do for a living?" he asked.

"I work for the Anglican Church."

"Doing what?"

"They employ me to try and persuade people to be Christians."

"My mate just became a Christian. He goes to the Baptist Church."

"Do you ever go to church?" I asked.

"I used to but haven't for a long time. I believe in God though."

"Great!"

"I sometimes say my prayers," he said. (I got the distinct impression that he thought I would be impressed.)

"When do you do that?" I enquired.

"Generally when I'm in trouble!" he replied.

I smiled. How well I knew that reaction. I'd done it a hundred times myself. Always when I was in trouble. "O God, if you will get me out of this jam, I'll . . ." I'd never kept the promise. I guess I'd never really meant to! Although I felt as though I did mean it at the time, when the crisis passed I always forgot the promise. There was no real friendship between God and me, not on my part anyway.

"I get upset when people treat me like that, don't you?" I asked.

"What do you mean?" He sounded surprised and puzzled.

"I'm usually upset when people only want me because they are in trouble or when they want to use me in one way or another."

There was a long silence, but he didn't say any more. I thought again, what strange mixtures we are. We hate it when people cultivate us to use us, yet when we do it to God, we think He will be happy.

It is a thoroughly unsatisfactory way to treat God and again I had passed judgment on myself by my reaction to that young man. I seem to be able to recognise inconsistency in others faster than I can recognise it in myself.

If only He wasn't always right

I'm at a party. There is a large crowd and I start talking to a stranger who is near me. He is pleasant and makes me feel at ease. Having just read *Nicholas and Alexandra* by Robert K Massie, I hold forth on the horrors of the 1914–18 war and the Russian involvement in it. I might say that although that book constitutes the greater bulk of my knowledge of that event it does not stop me going on and on as if I am a specialist in the field. After about fifteen minutes, when I pause for breath, I ask my new 'friend' what he does for a living.

"I'm a lecturer at the university here," he replies.

"What faculty?"

"History."

"Ancient or modern?" (There might yet be hope!)

"Actually, I did my thesis on the Russian involvement in the 1914-18 war." (Wouldn't you know it?)

What do I do now? He has given me a valuable piece of information. Up to now I have assumed that I am a specialist (on the basis of having read one paperback). What course of action can I take?

I have several options open to me. I can talk about the weather or the football. I can continue to hold forth as if I really *do* know what I'm talking about, when, in fact, I'm an amateur. Or I can admit that I've been talking through my hat and get him, from his knowledge as a specialist, to tell me what the true picture really was. One thing is certain, if there is to be any positive relationship between us then I will have to stop pretending I am his equal (at least in the area of history). I need to recognise that he knows more than I do. If I don't do that but continue as if I know as much about the subject as he does, you can be sure when he goes home he will say to his wife, "Who was that crashing bore?" However, if I let him share with me from his knowledge, there is no reason in the world why we shouldn't become friends. Indeed if we do, there is a good chance that I will really learn something about that part of history. The whole relationship will have a broadening effect on me. He will teach me from his resources what I could never know if left to myself.

All relationships work like this. When I know more than you do on a given subject then you recognise that, and you act appropriately. When you know more than I do, the reverse takes place — and when we are mutually ignorant, we will have lively discussions. But if I pretend to be a specialist, when, in fact, I'm an amateur, you can be sure that I will be a crashing bore.

When I encountered Christianity and began to understand what it was really about, one of my biggest problems was right at that point — I didn't want God to be *God*. At least not over me. I didn't mind the idea that God should be God over everyone else. In fact, I rather liked that idea. I just didn't want Him to be God over me. I wasn't too sure if I wanted to relate to someone who really *was* a specialist in everything. The truth was that I tried to relate to God as if He wasn't a specialist at all. I didn't think it a strange thing to tell God that He was quite wrong in His views of life — all rather old-fashioned really, I thought — and the idea of submitting my life to Him never occurred to me. If it had, it would have been quickly dealt with. I was going to be free and submit to no one. That attitude could only make me into a very lonely man. I needed to have within me, all the available resources for life.

Several years ago I worked in a church in London. In the congregation was an artist named Tim.

"Have you been to the National Gallery?" he asked.

"Yes. It's a truly marvellous collection."

"Did you see the seventeenth century Dutch paintings?"

"If I did, Tim, I didn't take them in."

"Can I take you to the Gallery sometime and show them to you?"

What are my options? I can submit to him as a specialist or, alternatively, resent his expertise and say, "I'm really terribly busy Tim but if I find a moment I'll let you know."

I did, in fact, go with him. Those who know that marvellous room in the Gallery will know what a feast was in store for me. I had missed it. It is only a small room, with small canvases, not brightly coloured, not the type which would have immediately caught my attention.

"Do you know what this painter is trying to do?" Tim asked.

"Tell me," I replied. "I really know nothing about it." Out of his lifetime study, Tim began to explain to me what was really there before my eyes. It was as if I had been blind. We were there for only an hour, yet a whole world opened for me.

It is not an exaggeration to say that I wasn't the same man. Whenever I had a spare minute I slipped back to the Gallery and sat in that room. I am sure you will have had similar experiences, maybe not in regard to art, but perhaps in other areas. It may have been in bush walking, when after having been taken to a particularly beautiful spot, you've gone back many times. You might have stumbled onto it yourself, but you didn't, someone shared it with you. It was part of friendship. You might have been shown a special surfing technique which has increased your enjoyment of the sport. It was part of friendship.

What a strange mixture we are. How could I get it so right with my friends and yet be so wrong when it came to God. At best I treated Him like an equal — at my worst I treated Him as if I knew better than He did. I pushed Him away, kept Him at arm's length and wouldn't let Him share His world or His life with me. I never really thought it out but it was as if I were saying, "I am a completely resourceful man. I don't need your friendship."

Caught in my own net

The ways I set out to relate to God were ways which irritated me when people tried them on me. I hated it when I was ignored and treated like a block of wood. I did not respond happily when I was used and manipulated. I found it a 'pain-in-the-neck' when people raved on in areas where they didn't really know what they were talking about. I was caught in my own net.

I had ignored God and just gone on as if He wasn't there. I had used Him. In times of great crises I had said my prayers with accompanying promises. I had stood up to God and had corrected Him when I felt Him to be in error. I was not really a friend of God.

I know that I am not unique in this.

But why are we like this?

CHAPTER THREE

Something is Terribly Wrong

We only need to reflect on the world around us to know that something is radically wrong. We aren't very good at solving our problems. At least, not the ones which have to do with people. In the international arena we seem better at getting into strife than in getting out of it.

I was fifteen years old when the second World War ended. It, like the first World War, was the war to end all wars. What high sounding words they were! They seem strange to our ears now in the light of Suez, Korea, Cuba, Vietnam, the Middle East, Kampuchea, Northern Ireland, Hungary, Poland, The Falklands and the whole East-West confrontation with its escalating arms race. It's a fact that we aren't terribly good at living with one another in this world.

Yet what is written large on the international scene is just slightly smaller on our national one. Although we are often told in Australia that our industrial record is no worse than most western countries, all I can say is it must be 'murder' in those countries where it is worse. In one year in one state of Australia, we had for longer or shorter periods, a postal workers' strike, an electricity strike, rail strike, garbage workers' strike, sewerage workers' strike and petrol carters' strike. There may have been others but those were the ones which affected me most. In fact, such strikes have become such a way of life that we have learned to live with them and in some cases we've found workable alternatives. I'm not saying workers shouldn't strike, nor am I going into the merits of particular groups. I am only making the point that we are not very good at solving our problems.

When we get to the smaller unit of society, the family, we find that the same problems exist. They just don't get the same publicity. I have been interested to see people's reaction when we talk about marriage and family life. In most cases people simply say, "It certainly didn't turn out the way I thought it would." For some it is better than they had hoped, but for most it is plain hard work.

Why do we have to work so hard to keep good things good? Why do good things sour so easily unless they are constantly cultivated? Why in an argument is it easier to say something hard, cruel and biting than to say something calming and conciliatory? Negative reactions and attitudes just seem to come naturally to me, and I suspect I am not unique! How often I said, "I will not fight with my father again." Those encounters were so unpleasant. I hated them and I am sure he hated them too. Yet I seemed powerless to deal with them. I knew in our family that if we were unselfish and looked out for the interests of each other we would be a happier group, yet I persisted in believing that if I could get my own way I would be happy. I had no trouble coping with this inconsistency. *Why are we like that?*

Even when we reach rock bottom and are alone, we still find the same struggle. We are often frightened when we meet new people and new situations. We are not at peace within ourselves. We worry about what people think about us. We lose our tempers. We lack self-control and have low self-esteem. *Why is it so?*

Not the total picture
Having said all that, I know it is not the total picture, nor is it a balanced view. Life is not totally grim. From time to time I find myself surprised by my ability to do something quite helpful — and sometimes I seem able to do it spontaneously. I see around me people making self-

sacrificing efforts to help others and I have to say, "This is a good world in which to live."

Nations, as well as individuals, rise to great heights of achievement in positive benefits to mankind. I have read a report recently of a major breakthrough in research into multiple sclerosis. What a marvellous thing that would be. However, it is indeed marvellous that people are actually working in the area at all. Then the power goes off because of the electricity workers' strike, and I am reminded that the total picture is that the good and the bad are muddled together.

Within the family situation I have known such great moments of love, tenderness and forgiveness, understanding and trust, that I have said, "It's good to be alive!" I've stood in parts of the world where my breath has been caught by the beauty and grandeur of the scenery. For several years I lived in Moree, a country town in northern New South Wales. Those western plains were so flat that ninety percent of the scenery before me seemed to be sky. I used to wait eagerly for evening to come. The sunsets were so brilliant, and night after night the whole sky lit up in blazing colour. "What a great place this is to live" was my attitude. I had the same reaction when I stood for the first time on Seven Mile Beach and saw the golden sand and the blue sea and miles of rolling breakers. I have experienced the exhilaration of coming in like a torpedo on a wave in the surf and saying, "It's good to be alive!"

Very early one morning I left Bombay in a bus for the airport. People were sleeping in the streets and on the footpaths. Rubbish and manure were everywhere. There was a terrible stench. I knew that some of the bodies were dead and others were dying and I was appalled. I said to a man next to me, "This is the worst sight I have ever seen."

"You obviously haven't been to Calcutta," he responded. "I was only saying to my wife how clean this city is compared with Calcutta."

I felt sick and said, "What a hopelessly mucked up world this is."

The true picture is that it is both good and bad — muddled is the right description. I can pretend it is all good or I can do the opposite. It is possible to act like a child and simply close my eyes to the problems and pretend I have caused them to disappear. On the other hand I can become constantly depressed by only concentrating on the bad parts. The only way forward is to live in the real world. But again I want to ask the question, *Why is it so?*

It isn't really good enough
Having recognised it as it is, I want to cry out, "It's not really good enough." The good parts are too infrequent and I have to work so hard to get to them and keep them. Sometimes I cannot do anything about the situation in which I find myself. I have a friend who has cerebral palsy, and it seems to take him ages to simply say, "Good morning." He is a university graduate and has a fine mind locked in an uncontrollable body. He is a spastic. It's not really good enough!

Why is it so?
The Bible has an explanation. It is in the book of Genesis, the first book of the Bible. This book tells about the beginning of the world. A great deal of debate has taken place as to whether this ancient book is meant to be history or is to be taken figuratively. It is not my intention to enter into that debate in this book, but whichever is the right way, the message of Genesis is clear, indeed only too clear.

Before we look at what it says, it may be helpful to say that the Bible's preoccupation with the creation story is with *who* and *why* rather than with *how*. 'How it works and what we can do with it' is the preoccupation of the scientific age. We hardly ever get around to asking, "Who did it?" and even less frequently do we ask the question, "Why was it done?" I remember when I first saw a bowling alley, pins were being scattered, gathered, sorted and placed back into position. I said to the person with me, "How do you think it works?" Even to this day I haven't bothered to find out who invented it.

The Bible has a different perspective. Its interest is in *who* created the world and *why*. We really need to remember that, and not expect the Bible to do what its writers never intended, that is to give scientific information.

Everything in the garden was lovely

In chapter one of the book Genesis, the writer tells us that God created everything and that God created mankind to have dominion over the creation. He doesn't tell us *how* God did it, but *that* He did it. The writer describes it like this:

"Then God said, 'Let us make man in our image, in our likeness, and let them rule over the fish of the sea and the birds of the air, over the livestock, over all the earth, and over all the creatures that move along the ground.' So God created man in his own image, in the image of God he created him; male and female he created them. God blessed them and said to them. 'Be fruitful and increase in number; fill the earth and subdue it. Rule over the fish of the sea and the birds of the air and over every living creature that moves on the ground.' . . . God saw all that he had made, and it was very good." (Genesis 1:26-28,31).

In chapter two, marriage is instituted and at the end of that chapter there is the beautiful statement, "The man and his wife were both naked, and they felt no shame." (Genesis 2:25) I do not really think this statement has much to do with sexuality. This is a statement about relationships. They were both completely honest with each other. They were both completely known by each other and neither one was a threat to the other.

They had nothing to hide. It is a description of a perfect relationship.

I have a friend who has two sons who were born eighteen months apart. When they get into a scrap, the older boy, being a bit bigger, always gets the better of his younger brother. However, the younger has a trump card which he plays when defeat is staring him in the face. He simply says to his brother, "Get off *now* or I'll tell them at school you still take your teddy to bed with you." It has never failed. Big brother is reduced to a quivering mass and leaps off as if he is spring-loaded, for unlike the woman and the man in Genesis 2, when he is "naked" he *is* ashamed. We all know that experience. We have all said and done things which we don't want anyone to find out about, and to be "naked" is to be ashamed.

By the time the writer of Genesis comes to the end of chapter two, he describes an idyllic world in which people are in friendship with God. They are not threatened by God or by each other or by the world around them. They live harmoniously under God's authority. They live in the garden of Eden and are allowed full authority except in one area. In the middle of the garden is a tree designated "the tree of the knowledge of good and evil" the fruit of which is forbidden to Adam and Eve, and added to the restriction is a penalty, "when you eat of it you will surely die".

The message is crystal clear. God created the world; God created people; He gave them a wonderful world in which to live; He set them in authority over His world and He did all this on purpose so that they could exercise authority under His authority. He gave them ample opportunity to demonstrate their love and thankfulness to Him. There was almost no restriction placed on them, indeed only enough so that they should be morally responsible people.

At the end of chapter two of Genesis, everything in the garden is lovely, but it is hardly a picture of the world in which we are living today and by the time we get to the end of chapter three of Genesis, everything has fallen apart. People are threatening and being threatened by each other. They are threatened by their environment, and they are threatening and are being threatened by God. Marriage is under strain. Work is now hard and often a drudgery.

The idyllic world has been wrecked and has become the world with which we are completely familiar. The good still lingers on and is muddled with the bad. What went wrong and why is it so?

Who will be God?

In Genesis chapter three we are introduced in God's creation to an evil supernatural being in the form of the serpent. This story is simple and universal, but we are mistaken if we think it is not profound. It begins like this:

Now the serpent was more crafty than any of the wild animals the Lord God had made. He said to the woman, "Did God really say, 'You must not eat from any tree in the garden'?" (Genesis 3:1) [See what is implied? He is suggesting that God is mean and does not care about people.]

The woman said to the serpent, "We may eat fruit from the trees in the garden, but God did say, 'You must not eat fruit from the tree that is in the middle of the garden, and you must not touch it, or you will die'." (Genesis 3:2,3). [You can almost hear the serpent saying, "She must be the original dumb blond!"]

"You will not surely die," the serpent said to the woman. "For God knows that when you eat of it your eyes will be opened, and you will be like God, knowing good and evil." (Genesis 3:4,5).

Notice the full impact of this temptation. She is called on to do three things: 1. To doubt God's word; 2. To doubt God's judgment; 3. To doubt God's goodness.

1. *Doubt God's word.* The woman is called upon to disbelieve what God has so clearly said. The serpent suggests

that not only will she not die, but in fact she will become like God Himself. She will be totally independent of God. She will be able to decide herself what is good and evil. Being now a law maker by right she need never be a law breaker. A very appealing idea. We all love it. We, like the woman, have all believed it and have set ourselves up as our own authorities not under God but against God. God has become a rival, not a friend.

2.   *Doubt God's judgment.* She is tempted to believe that the consequences of this action will not bring judgment upon her. "You will not die," the serpent says. "Don't worry about the consequences. Nothing will happen. Live for now. Tomorrow will take care of itself. You *will be God yourself.*"

The idea that our actions can be isolated from their results is very appealing. The owner of an aching head and heaving stomach following a party the night before, would find it irresistable. We would prefer to choose to do as we like, and to choose the outcome of our actions as well, but that cannot be done.

3.   *Doubt God's goodness.* Eve is called upon to doubt that God has her best interests at heart. The serpent is really saying, "God doesn't really want the best for you. He has got much better things but He's not going to let you have them. If you want the best out of life grab it and run. God is the number one kill-joy. He is completely self-interested. He doesn't want anyone else to be God, but you can easily outsmart Him. You can 'out-God' Him at His own game."

That seems to be a reasonably true description of the way we all respond to God. We set ourselves up as authorities in His world, and we rebel against what He says. We feel ourselves at liberty to rewrite the rules and, what's more, we do not give a moment's thought to the consequences.

Some people fiddle with their income tax returns. Others carry on with someone else's husband or wife. Many who are in business, feel they cannot be honest *and* successful. We all say, "It's my life . . . I'll run it my way." We think we have come of age and can properly dispense with anything which God might have said. He is old-fashioned. It is a universal story. Notice how it continues:

> When the woman saw that the fruit of the tree was good for food and pleasing to the eye, and also desirable for gaining wisdom, she took some and ate it. She also gave some to her husband, who was with her and he ate it. (Genesis 3:6)

How very appealing it all was! Good for food and pleasant to look at. In a summary the serpent redefines the good life in terms of good food, intellectual stimulation and the arts. He offers the woman a truly liberated life of self-indulgence which he claims will bring her to maturity of personality. But best of all, the fruit was "desirable for gaining wisdom". "You will be as God", the serpent said, and non-stop the words rang in her ears: "I'll be God. I'll be God. I'll be the most important person in the world, number one."

It would surprise me if you don't have the same problem. I certainly do. I think I'm such a clever person. I cannot work out why everyone else doesn't see it too!

It's lonely being God

Now the trouble with setting ourselves up as God is that everyone is a threat to us and we are alone. If I am pretending to be God and so are you, what will happen when we meet? Which one of us will be God? We see this illustrated for us by children as they play. Most of them have the subtlety of a train smash at ninety kilometres an hour. So if the one who owns the bat does not get his own way, he simply takes his bat home. But that really isn't what he wants — he wants to play cricket, but for that he needs others. He wants his own way, and if he can't get it, he will not play. It is lonely being God when everyone else wants to be God.

I heard recently about a young man who played rugby union in a church team. They needed him to make up the fifteen members and they could not field a team without him. "Sure, I'll play," he said, "provided I play lock. I won't play if I can't play lock." It's the same principle. If you won't let me be God, I'm going home. However, it hardly ever leads to a good relationship with others.

As adults we learn to get our own way by more subtle means than falling on the ground in a tantrum. We do it by manipulating those around us. In the ancient world the worst thing which could happen to you was for your brother to become emperor. Hy systematically eliminated all possible rivals, and since he could never be sure which of his brothers might try to overthrow him, he generally started on all the members of the family, just to be on the safe side. It is lonely at the top.

The Genesis story proceeds like this:

> Then the eyes of both of them were opened, and they realised they were naked; so they sewed fig leaves together and made coverings for themselves. (Genesis 3:7)

I'm sure that was a great solution! Compare this with the earlier statement, "The man and his wife were both naked, and they felt no shame." Now that they have disobeyed God, that relationship is under threat. For the first time they are afraid of each other. They realise they are vulnerable. They try to hide from each other, yet the way they do it shows their inability to cope. I am sure the writer wants us to laugh like the proverbial drain pipe at the fig leaves! I must say that the paintings and statues I have seen with such fig leaves, the coverings seem very insubstantial. Before you laugh too much, ask yourself if it is not the perfect picture of us. We want to be able to share our lives with others. We want close friendship and deep love. We need someone to whom we can tell our secret longings and our inmost fears yet we are frightened to do so in case they turn on us and 'tell them at school we still take our teddy to bed'. We are frightened, but the covering we make is really inadequate to deal with the situation. The story might be simple, but it is not childish.

The first consequence of disobedience to God is that we are a threat to each other. We want and need each other, yet we are frightened to give ourselves in genuine commitment. It's lonely being God when you're not God.

Enemies of God

The second consequence of the man and the woman turning their backs on God is that they are now frightened of God and they try to run away from Him. However, they are no good at that either.

> Then the man and his wife heard the sound of the Lord God as he was walking in the garden in the cool of the day, and they hid from the Lord God among the trees of the garden. But the Lord God called to the man, 'Where are you?'
>
> He answered, 'I heard you in the garden, and I was afraid because I was naked, so I hid.'
>
> And he said, 'Who told you that you were naked? Have you eaten from the tree that I commanded you not to eat from?' (Genesis 3:8-11)

We have here the picture of God seeking friendship with mankind. He comes to them in the cool of the day to relax and have fellowship with them. I think the writer wishes us to see that this was not a new thing, but something which had happened regularly before. But something quite new is introduced. Not only are they threatened by each other, but now they are threatened by God. Their friendship is turned into enmity. They try to hide from God but can't really do that any more than they could hide from each other.

We, like they, find ourselves wanting to live independently from God, yet we come up against situations where we call on God to help us. We want to hide and we don't want God to find us or tell us how to live, yet we cannot do that, not all the time, and not consistently.

Blind to their danger

The third consequence of their rebellion is that they become quite blind to their situation. In any broken friendship there is only one way for it to be repaired. The guilty party or parties need to admit their mistake and ask for forgiveness.

Given God's goodness to the man and his wife, you would have expected that to His question, "Have you eaten from the tree that I commanded you not to eat from?", they would have come out into the open, admitting their mistake, asking for forgiveness and seeking reconciliation. However, they are quite blind to their danger. Believing themselves to be equal with God they stand up to Him and actually blame Him for their folly. This is not the way of reconciliation.

The man said, "The woman you put here with me, she gave me some fruit from the tree, and I ate it." (Genesis 3:12) He is virtually saying, "I didn't ask for the woman. You can't hold me responsible for her." It is the first statement of a theme to be repeated often — "Am I my brother's keeper?" [There is still hope. The woman might yet confess, apologise and seek to restore the broken relationship.]

Then the Lord God said to the woman, "What is this you have done?" The woman said, "The serpent deceived me, and I ate," (Genesis 3:13) Don't fail to notice the import of this statement. She is saying that God is really to blame. "I can't help it if you allowed the serpent to be so clever that he can trick anyone." She wants to be God in one breath and not take the responsibilities for her actions in the next. Yet I know exactly how she felt. I too have known that blindness and inconsistency.

What is the way out?
From that moment the consequences of their action of rebellion became plain.

Enmity exists between the evil powers and mankind (Genesis 3:15). Marriage is under threat and now needs to be worked at to maintain it (Genesis 3:16); work becomes hard because the environment is not always friendly to mankind (Genesis 3:17-19), and finally mankind is separated from God and the garden. Man cannot, by himself, get back again (Genesis 3:22-24). Now this can only happen if God takes action in some way to help them in their plight. The rest of the Bible is taken up with the whole record of how God does just that.

He sets out to rescue us in our plight.

Before we leave the story of Adam and Eve, I want to point out that it is the story of every person's rebellion. In one way or another we too have rebelled against God. It might have been by simply ignoring His overtures of friendship. It might have been by seeking to use Him when in trouble or by just standing up to Him as if we were His equal. In one or all of these ways, we have exercised our independence of God by rebelling against Him.

Who fired the most shots?
When our rebellion toward God is active and open, we know it. However, when our rebellion is a state of passive indifference, if we bother to think about it we probably think it isn't so real. Some people have quite openly said to me, "I haven't rebelled against God."

"What do you do about Him then?" I've asked.

"Nothing. I just ignore Him."

Suppose we are both soldiers in trench warfare. You have a single firing rifle. I have an automatic sub-machine gun of the latest variety. The enemy charges us and we both blast off with maximum potential. There is no doubt that I will fire more shots than you will. Suppose we are both captured. No one will ask, "Who fired the most

shots?'' We will both be treated like enemies because that
is what we are. The question is really one of whose side
we are on. Some of us have demonstrated our rebellion
by the automatic sub-machine gun method. Others do it
by the single firing method, and there are others who
are back at the base boiling the billy for the rest. However, the Bible says we have all rebelled.

God's plan for reconciliation

We couldn't really have blamed God if He had left us to
'stew in our own juice', but that is not the way He is nor
is it the way He acts. In spite of our rejection of Him,
God has never stopped caring for His creation. He took
action to effect our rescue.

The Bible is about God's plan to bring about a reconciliation between Himself and mankind, between people
and people, and ultimately to bring all His people into a
new environment — one which is not hostile to them.
God did this by choosing a nation to whom He would
reveal both Himself and His plan to save the world.

At the end of Genesis chapter two, we are shown a
picture of God's people, living in God's place, under God's
rule. At the end of Genesis chapter three, this has been
reversed. The people have set themselves up as enemies
to God. They have been excluded from the garden and
they are rebellious to God's rule.

One man — one nation — one man

The unfolding plan of God began with His call to a man
in ancient times, to Abraham. He was to be God's man
and to live under His rule, and God promised him that
He would make him into a great nation, that He would
give that nation a land to live in and that through them,
all the peoples in the world would be blessed (Genesis
12:1-3). God would, as it were, start again with Abraham
and his descendants, and He made an agreement with
them.

Although Abraham did not live to see the fulfilment of that promise, in time his descendants grew in number into the people we call the Jews. They in time settled in Canaan, having been rescued from Egypt where they were slaves. This was done by an intervention of God and by God's chosen leaders, Moses and Joshua.[1] In Canaan, as the nation of Israel, they were to live again as God's people, under God's rule, in God's place. It was to be a new 'garden of Eden'. However, they did no more than approximate to that. Most of the time they rebelled against God's rule and were overrun by enemies. Again and again God raised up leaders who were able to rescue the Jews from this situation. These saviours were not able to bring about any permanent peace because the people continued to rebel against God.[2]

In time God provided them with kings who were to lead and rule the people in such a way that all the neighbouring nations would know what it was like to live under God's leadership. The king was to represent God to the people. He was to serve them and rescue them from their enemies. During this time God progressively revealed to His people His own character. Moses the law-giver and prophets were sent to call the Jews back to obedience under the terms of the agreement made between God and the Jewish nations.[3] Under king David and through his son, Solomon, the Jews probably came closer to living like God's people than at any other time. This, however, was only temporary and after the death of Solomon, the nation was divided through civil war, and under such powerful nations as Babylon, Assyria, Greece and Rome, the Jews again became a slave nation.[4]

The history of the Jews during that long time is one of lost opportunities. Again and again, they were unable — because of their disobedience and unbelief — to re-

1. You can read about this in the following books of the Bible: Genesis, Exodus, Deuteronomy, Joshua.
2. You can read about this in Judges.
3. You can read about this in Leviticus, Isaiah, Amos.
4. You can read about this in 1 and 2 Samuel and Jeremiah.

spond to God properly in the special relationship in which He had placed them. The promised land was no 'Garden of Eden'. From Abraham onwards no one responded to God with the same love He had shown towards them.

Every now and again it seemed possible to hope that there would be someone, somehow, who would obey God and reverse the situation, but each time that hope faded. It became apparent that if God were to bring about a permanent rescue for His people, something new needed to be done.

Through His prophets, God promised He would send a new leader — one who would bring about a permanent peace. He would be a true king to God's people; He would be their shepherd. These hopes for a Messiah (anointed one), grew as God gave more promises about the coming king.[1]

Finally that new king arrived in the person of Jesus. God's plan narrowed once again into one person, His Son Jesus, who came to provide a permanent reconciliation between God the Father and His creation, mankind; between people and people, and ultimately between people and the rest of God's creation, their environment.

Unlike the others, Jesus did not let His opportunity slip away. He obeyed God and lived out the implications of the special relationship between God and His people. Consequently He is the climax of God's plan to rescue us.[2]

1. Some of these promises are found in: Isaiah 9:6,7; 11:1-11; Jeremiah 23:5,6; Ezekiel 34; Daniel 7:9-14.
2. See *The Gospel and the Kingdom;* Graeme Goldsworthy. Paternoster Press 1981.

CHAPTER FOUR

What has God Done About it?

Jesus is at the centre of God's rescue plan. It can only be understood as we understand Jesus, and to help us to do that, we must look at the following questions about Him.
1. Why was Jesus born?
2. Why did Jesus die?
3. Why did Jesus rise from the dead?
4. What is Jesus doing now?
5. Why will Jesus return again?

Having answered those questions, we should be in a good position to understand God's intention for us and how we should act.

1. WHY WAS JESUS BORN?

I suppose of all the stories of Jesus, the ones about His birth are the best known. We have all heard about Mary and Joseph going back to Bethlehem to be enrolled for the census, and how because there was no room in the inn, Mary gave birth to Jesus in a stable, wrapped the new born babe in swaddling cloths and placed him in a manger. We have heard about the shepherds and the wise men, and most of us have been in a Christmas play when we were children.

Luke recorded the story of the visit of the angel Gabriel, God's messenger, to Mary and described the role of the child she would bear in these words: "He will be great and will be called the Son of the Most High. The Lord God will give him the throne of his father David, and he will reign over the house of Jacob for ever; his kingdom will never end" (Luke 1:32,33).

The angel told Mary that Jesus was to be that promised king, the one who would bring about a permanent salvation. The birth is highly significant. God's promise made thousands of years before, was fulfilled in the coming of Jesus. He and He alone is ruler over God's world. Don't let the significance escape you. If Jesus is such a king, what will happen to me if I continue to reject His rule and rebel against Him? It is obviously serious.

In the message of the angels to the shepherds of Bethlehem, Luke's Gospel gives us a further insight into why Jesus was born: "I bring you good news of great joy that will be for all people. Today in the town of David a Saviour has been born to you; he is Christ the Lord" (Luke 2:10,11). This tells us some more about Jesus. Not only is He to be king in God's world, but He is to effect a rescue operation. That is why His coming is good news of great joy to all people. So great is the rescue operation of Jesus that not one person need be excluded. Its effect can flow on to all people.

For men and women who have turned away from God and have set themselves up as rivals to God in open rebellion, there is a way back to forgiveness, peace with God and life as God meant it to be. Jesus said, "I have come that you might have life and have it to the full" (John 10:10).

Again He said, "Come unto me, all you who are weary and burdened, and I will give you rest" (Matthew 11:28). It really is good news. Jesus has come to rescue us from ourselves. For the person who is sick of mucking up his life and everyone else's, there is good news. For those who say "Life is not good enough", there is good news. *You can be rescued from yourself.*

One night I saw a wonderful rescue operation shown 'live' on television. I turned on the late night news and learned that a small child had fallen down a nine inch bore hole. The tragedy was made more acute by the fact that only six months earlier a lad in northern Italy had died in a similar accident. I saw the child's parents in distress. Then a group of miners, who had heard about it over the radio, arrived by truck, equipped and ready to help. They knew exactly what to do, they bored a hole alongside and tunnelled in. At 10.30 p.m. I saw them at work. The announcer kept assuring us that at any moment the boy would be rescued. The child could do nothing. At 11.30 p.m. we were assured again that at any moment the boy would be rescued. At 1.05 a.m. I saw a miner winched up out of the hole with the small child in his arms. It was a very moving scene. Both the little boy and his rescuer were grinning from ear to ear. The parents were weeping tears of joy and, I guess, relief.

What a great moment that was. The danger had passed. The child was restored to his parents. What good news of great joy real rescues are!

Jesus did that for us.

But how did He do it? He did it through His death, and His coming back to life. This brings us to our second question.

2.   WHY DID JESUS DIE?
What Jesus thought

There can be no doubt that Jesus believed that His death was at the very centre of His work. Without it His mission would have been a failure. Again and again Jesus reminded His disciples of it. They were not able to understand the significance of it nor did they wish to speak of it. Yet Jesus persisted. Matthew wrote of an interesting exchange between Jesus and Peter:

> "From that time on Jesus began to explain to his disciples that he must go to Jerusalem and suffer many things at the hands of the elders, chief priests and teachers of the law, and that he must be killed and on the third day be raised to life.

> Peter took him aside and began to rebuke him. 'Never, Lord!' he said. 'This shall never happen to you!'

> Jesus turned and said to Peter: 'Out of my sight, Satan! You are a stumbling block to me; you do not

have in mind the things of God, but the things of men' " (Matthew 16:21-23).

The idea that God would send a saviour to die as Jesus claimed would happen, was so out of step with Peter's idea of a saviour, that he was unable to control himself. However, so central was it to God's plan for Jesus, that to suggest otherwise, was to be a mouthpiece for God's enemy, Satan.

The importance of Jesus' death can be gauged by this statement of His:

"The reason that the Father loves me is that I *lay down my life* — only to take it up again. No-one takes it from me, but I lay it down of my own accord. I have authority to lay it down and authority to take it up again. This command I received from my Father" (John 10:17,18).

After His death and resurrection, when Jesus appeared to His disciples, He explained to them that the Old Testament scriptures predicted that when God's Messiah came, His death would be at the centre of His work.

"Then he opened their minds so they could understand the Scriptures. He told them, 'This is what is written: The Christ will suffer and rise from the dead on the third day, and repentance and forgiveness of sins will be preached in his name . . .' " (Luke 24:45-47a).

For some people an untimely death can only be described as a terrible tragic waste; usually it comes in its normal course in the fulness of a ripe old age. In the life of Jesus it was seen as the very pivotal point of his achievements. It was because of His death that we are able to be reconciled to God. Jesus saw in His death the means whereby our sins could be forgiven. Very early in His ministry He had been reminded of this by John the Baptist who described Him as "the Lamb of God who takes away the sin of the world" (John 1:29).

Where did they get this idea?

There is no doubt that both John and Jesus had arrived at these ideas from their study of the Old Testament scriptures. Jesus tells us this of Himself (Luke 24:46). It is not possible to be certain which passages Jesus would have used to do this, but one of the clearest statements is found in the book of the prophet Isaiah in chapter fifty-three. Isaiah describes a servant of God who is upright and godly, and the prophet is disturbed because this righteous person is manhandled, mistreated and disfigured almost beyond recognition. It's not fair! What has he done? Why is he so "despised and rejected by men, a man of sorrows, and familiar with suffering" (Isaiah 53:3)? As the prophet ponders this sight, his insight is such that he realises that the victim is suffering, not for himself but for others. This is how he describes it,

"But he was pierced for our transgressions, he was crushed for our iniquities; the punishment that brought us peace was upon him, and by his wounds we are healed. We all, like sheep, have gone astray, each of us has turned to his own way; and the Lord has laid on him the iniquity of us all" (Isaiah 53:4-6).

The prophet sees the suffering of this godly servant of God to be the means whereby God will bring forgiveness to His people. This idea of a coming servant of God who would suffer on behalf of others was not ever understood correctly until Jesus came and did it Himself. He is the one on whom the punishment for our sins was laid.

What Jesus knew would happen by His death was that He would make a way whereby we can be forgiven and come back and be friends with God.

God's attitude to our rebellion

Up to now I have described the way in which our rebellion and indifference to God has affected us. We have seen it in terms of our inability to get on with each other, of not having God as a friend or being in a world which isn't always helpful to us. But now we need to think about the effect which our rebellion has had on God.

The Bible tells us that God is a person who loves what is right and hates what is wrong. Although He has offered me His friendship I have spurned it. Although He is God I have set myself up as a rival. I say to God, "I will run my own life my own way." However, the real trouble begins when I try to do just that. I cannot control history, I cannot control society nor indeed my own life. In our independence from God we have mucked up our own lives; we have mucked up each others lives and we have all made our contribution in mucking up the world in which we live.

This doesn't seem a very important thing to us because in our blindness, we believe we are the rightful masters in God's world. However, the Bible gives a totally different picture. God is not only the master and creator of His world but is also its moral judge. Unlike we, who often grow weary of old projects and abandon them, God has never wearied of His world. He cares about me and how I run my life — He loves me. He cares about you and how I treat you — He loves you. He cares about the world and how we treat it. It is not a matter of indifference to Him that injustice, oppression and suffering are the lot of millions of people. He is not indifferent to a world mucked up by our rebellion. The Bible calls our rebellion and indifference, sin. It is the great folly of mankind to believe that God doesn't really care about what happens to us. He hates sin because of its devastating effect. He hates sin because it is completely opposed to His character. "God is light and in him there is no darkness at all" is the way John describes Him (1 John 1:5). "Your eyes are too pure to look on evil; you cannot tolerate wrong" is the way Habakkuk describes God (Habakkuk 1:13).

God acts consistently

Our rebellion has had a marked effect on us. But it has had an even more serious effect on God. There is an apparent dilemma. On the one hand God declares His love for mankind, and on the other, He cannot, and will not, tolerate sin. This is resolved perfectly in the death of Jesus. If God simply said, "forget about your rebellion, it doesn't really matter" then the consequences would be too horrific to contemplate. From then on nothing would ever be wrong again. There would be no significant difference between a kindly act of love and the actions of two youths who kicked an old man to death in a bus shelter recently.

We feel, from time to time, that God should overlook our sins. But when we reflect on the enormous consequences, we will want to call out "Wrong is wrong. Black is not white. Don't change the rules." But then we whisper "Just change them for me." To which comes back the reply, "Don't worry. This is a secure world. I will not change the rules *anywhere* for *anyone*, for *any reason.* You can be sure I will act consistently with my character. I love righteousness and hate iniquity. It is because of this that you know exactly where you stand."

God's justice is not opposed to His love — nor is His love weakly sentimental, causing Him to turn a blind eye to sin. His love and His justice meet in the death of Jesus.

"God so *loved* the world that he *gave* his one and only Son that whoever believes in him shall *not perish* but have eternal life" (John 3:16).

"This pleases God our Saviour who wants all men to be saved and come to a knowledge of the truth. For there is one God and one mediator between God and men, the man Christ Jesus, who gave himself as a ransom for all men" (1 Timothy 2:3-6).

Between sinful people and a holy God stands Jesus, who through His death, opens up a way for friendship between us.

How does it work?
We need to look more closely at what took place at the death of Jesus. Peter, who previously had objected in

strong terms to the idea of Jesus' death, saw its full significance. Here is his description: "He himself bore our
sins in his body on the tree" (1 Peter 2:24). The punishment which was due to me was actually taken by Jesus.
He had lived a perfect life and so was in a position to do
that. He had no sins of His own, and so no punishment
was due to Him.

It is when I understand this that I am able to make
more sense out of the way the Gospel writers describe
the events on the day Jesus died. Mark writes in his Gospel, "At the sixth hour [12 noon] darkness came over
the whole land until the ninth hour [3 p.m.]. And at the
ninth hour Jesus cried out in a loud voice, ". . . My God,
my God, why have you forsaken me?' . . . With a loud
cry Jesus breathed his last. The curtain of the temple was
torn in two from top to bottom" (Mark 15:33,37,38).

In symbolic gestures the blackness of the event is demonstrated by the sun being darkened. The Father who
always loved His one and only Son turned His back on
Jesus, as He who had never sinned, became sin for us.
The full weight of God's righteous anger against sin was
allowed to fall on Jesus, and He underwent our hell for
us so that we could be with Him in heaven. Jesus knew
what it was to be in the God-forsaken state — to be truly
cut off from God, and that is something which you and
I have never known. But that death was not purposeless.

The curtain was ripped apart

A little background information might help. The Jews
had an elaborate system of worship which was conducted
in the temple at Jerusalem. Certain parts of the temple
were open to all, while other parts were open only to
male Jews. In the centre of the temple was a place called
the Holy of Holies, and only one person was ever allowed
in there. He was the High Priest and was only allowed in
once a year. The Holy of Holies symbolised the presence
of God with His people. The fact that only the High

Priest was able to enter into God's presence and then only once a year and only after the most elaborate ritual, was a clear statement to the Jews, that:

"God cannot be approached easily by sinful man." Something needed to be done.

A curtain separated the Holy of Holies from the rest of the temple. Do you see the significance of the statement in Mark 15:38? When Jesus died His sinbearing death, He opened up a way of access into God's presence for anyone. The curtain was ripped apart.

Love and justice in harmony.

Imagine I am in court. I have broken the law. In fact, I was caught in the very act. At my trial, to my delight I discover the judge is an uncle of mine, in fact, my favourite uncle. What's more, I am a favourite of his. The trial proceeds yet I don't worry because I think my uncle will deal with me in the best way. My guilt is established and to my surprise I am sentenced by the judge to the maximum penalty. He loves all that is right and he will uphold the law! But what of friendship, kinship and love? Don't they mean anything? While I am being led away the clerk of the court hands me an envelope. You guessed it. In it is a cheque to pay the fine. It is from my uncle. In one action he upholds the law and so must punish me. He also takes the punishment in my place and thus demonstrates his love and concern for me.

In the death of Jesus, God has acted in a similar way. God condemns us for our rebellion but He allowed Jesus to take our punishment as a substitute so that we can be set free. His love and justice stay in perfect harmony.

This action of the death of Jesus is seen by the Bible writers to be the great demonstration of God's love to us. If you ask the question, "How much does God love us?" Paul the apostle, answers:

"Very rarely will anyone die for a righteous man, though for a good man someone might possibly dare to die. But God demonstrates his love for us in this: while we were still sinners, Christ died for us" (Romans 5:7,8). He loved His enemies.

God and the Lord Jesus Christ were in agreement in this action. They both loved us in the same way. It would be wrong to picture a stern, unmoved God being appeased by the loving Son. The Bible shows that both the Father and the Son were in complete agreement about their plan to bring us back into right relationship with them. It is described like this: "All this is from God, who reconciled us to himself through Christ" (2 Corinthians 5:18).

Many ways to describe it

So important is the death of Jesus and its effect for us, that the Bible writers use many different descriptions to help us see the true significance. In his letter to the Romans, the Apostle Paul, used three different ideas to help us understand it.

". . . for all have sinned and fall short of the glory of God, and are *justified* freely by his grace through the *redemption* that came by Christ Jesus. God presented him as a *sacrifice of atonement*, through faith in his blood . . ."(Romans 3:23-25a).

Paul begins by reminding us that we have all sinned. Not only have we said and done wrong things, but such actions spring from a rebellious spirit towards God. That rebellious spirit must be dealt with. If we all had a list of our wrong actions and we compared our lists, we would find some people's lists were longer than others. Some would contain actions not found in other lists, but whatever the state of those lists we know that their owners are equally rebellious in their hearts towards God. We just demonstrate rebellion in different ways.

Having reminded us of our dilemma, Paul uses three technical terms to describe the way in which the death of Jesus deals with it.

(a) *justification*
(b) *redemption*
(c) *sacrifice of atonement*

(a) A law court

"justified freely by his grace". Justification is a legal term and it means "to be declared to be in the right". In this context it means that we can be treated just-as-if we had never sinned.

I imagine myself in the dock on the day of judgment. I am standing before the moral judge of all the world. I know Him to be the Lord God Almighty. He loves justice and hates sin. I know myself to be a sinful person. I begin to ponder the full extent of the evidence which could be mustered against me. Open acts of rebellion committed against the living God. I can remember many of my sins only too clearly. Lapses in morality, in purity, honesty, truthfulness, times when I had opportunity to do good and which I neglected. I remember the times when I have condemned behaviour in others which I had sanctioned in myself. These are the evidences of a rebellious spirit towards God. Goodness only knows how many I have forgotten. I know I am guilty. I have not loved God with my heart, mind, soul and strength to say nothing of loving my neighbour as myself. The trouble with guilt is you can't undo it. It's happened! My plight is hopeless!

The preliminaries of my case are dispensed with. The Judge, to my great surprise, and I may say, delight, dismisses the case. 'This man is to be acquitted. He is to be treated just as if he had been innocent.' Staggering, isn't it? Yet this is exactly what Paul says, we ". . . are justified freely by his grace. . .through faith in his blood [death]." Because Jesus has died for me, I can be given the status of a justified man. I will be treated by God just-as-if I'd never sinned. This same idea is put forward by the apostle John. He says, ". . . if anybody does sin, we have one who speaks to the Father in our defence, Jesus Christ the Righteous One. He is the atoning sacrifice for our sins, and not only for ours but also for the sins of the world" (1 John 2:1,2).

(b) Slavery

"the redemption that comes by Jesus Christ". Redemption is a term used to buy someone out of slavery.

Imagine you are living in the ancient world. You have fallen into serious debt. There is no way out. You have lost everything. You have recourse only to one line of action. You sell yourself and your family into slavery. But you have a friend. He too is poor but he works day and night at anything and everything, year in and year out. He sacrifices and goes without. He deprives himself and even his children and on a day of unbelievable joy to you he buys you and your family from your owner and he sets you free.

Paul uses the term to show that through the death of Jesus we can be released from our slavery to sin and be set free. Not only can I be justified but I can be redeemed.

(c)   A sacrifice

"a sacrifice of atonement". The third illustration Paul uses in this passage to describe the effect of the death of Jesus is drawn from the sacrificial temple worship. We cannot be sure whether Paul is referring to the Jewish system or some pagan ritual. Probably the former.

The idea is clear. An animal was sacrificed in a symbolic action on behalf of the offender. The symbolism was twofold. It said "I deserve what is happening to the animal" and "I transfer my offence to this animal." Making such a sacrifice was *intended* to cause God's righteous anger to be averted. Paul is saying that because of the death of Jesus, God's righteous anger against us for our rebellion, can be averted. "God presented him as a sacrifice of atonement, through faith in his blood [death]" (Romans 3:25).

We are not unused to this idea of people sacrificing themselves on behalf of others. Sometimes we use the term 'supreme sacrifice' of men who died in war on behalf of others who lived. In Dickens' novel *The Tale of Two Cities* Sydney Carton substituted himself for his friend Charles Darnay who was in prison. He visited him on the night before his execution. Because they looked so much alike, Darnay was able to escape in Carton's clothes. Carton was executed the following day in the place of his friend — a great sacrifice.

An act of great sacrifice and heroism took place in Washington D.C. on January 14th 1982. A 737 plane crashed into the 14th Street Bridge and then sank into the icy Potomac River. Of the seventy-nine passengers only five persons were rescued from the disaster. This was done by pulling people out of the water with a line attached to a helicopter. The survivors all told the same story. Each had been handed the life line in the water by a man who had it first, yet when the helicopter finally returned for him he had disappeared and drowned while saving them.

Jesus sacrificed Himself for us, taking the full punishment which our sins deserved.

It really is important

The full impact of the death of Jesus should not be allowed to escape us. The more I ponder it the more significant it seems. I have never felt myself to be a very sinful person. However, I have come to see how important my rebellion against God is, by the great lengths to which he went to have them removed. If He allowed His one and only Son to die for me then it must be important. Those of you who are parents will see how much it matters by asking the simple question, "What event or circumstance could you imagine to be so important that you would let your child die for it?" It is mind boggling. Then know for a fact that God places the forgiveness of our sins in a very high category. It matters to Him so much that He *did* let His one and only Son die for us.

A paradox

The death of Jesus presents us with a paradox. It says two things which seem at first glance to be contradictory. On the one hand it says, "You matter to God" and on the other hand it says, "Your track record is very bad." Yet both are true.

Meditating on the death of Jesus helped me to understand these two truths. First, I am a highly significant person in God's eyes. I am not a nobody. God wishes me to be His friend — what a great privilege — and He does so knowing exactly what I am like. He persists even in the face of my rebellion. That is even more surprising. He sent His Son to die that I might be reconciled to Him. It is the great demonstration of His love.

"This is love, not that we loved God, but that he loved us and sent his Son as an atoning sacrifice for our sins" (1 John 4:10).

You may believe that you are an important person, or you may feel that you are insigificant and unnoticed. Know for a fact that you really *do* matter to God. The death of Jesus says so.

Not only does the death of Jesus show me how much God loves me, but it also shows me that my track record is very bad. If there had been some other way by which we could have been forgiven and made acceptable to God, then surely it would have been found.

The Gospel writers tell us of the deep agony of spirit that Jesus went through as He approached His sin-bearing death. In the garden of Gethsemane on the night before His death He prayed again and again, "My Father, if it be possible, may this cup be taken from me" (Mat-

thew 26:39). He had already explained to His disciples
"My soul is overwhelmed with sorrow to the point of
death". Luke tells us how that while He was at prayer,
". . . his sweat was like drops of blood falling to the
ground" (Luke 22:44).

We can be sure that the Father would certainly have
granted Jesus' request had it been possible. But it wasn't.

There was no other good enough
To pay the price of sin.
He only could unlock the gate
Of heaven, and let us in.

I have had to learn how serious my rebellion is and to
stop making light of it. It is obvious that God doesn't
dismiss it as being of no consequence.

Whatever would you say?
I was thinking about the plane which crashed into the
Potomac River in Washington. Seventy-four people were
killed. I never think of being killed when I travel by
plane. Some people do, but whether those people did, or
did not, by the end of that day they were in the presence
of God. Suppose you had been one of them and God
were to say to you, "What are you doing here unforgiven?" What ever would you say? "I've lived a good life"
or "I never got around to thinking about it" or "I didn't
think it mattered all that much?" Surely the answer would
come back — "You should have known better. Why ever
do you think I let my one and only Son die?"

3. WHY DID JESUS COME BACK FROM THE DEAD?
We have already seen that Jesus believed that it was
through His death that we could have our sins forgiven.
At the Last Supper, when Jesus spoke of His death, He
said, ". . . my blood . . . is poured out . . . for the
forgiveness of sins" (Matthew 26:28). His last words from
the cross were, "It is finished [accomplished]" (John
19:30), "Father, into your hands I commit my spirit"
(Luke 23:46).

Jesus believed that He had completed the work He had come to do. His death accomplished that. So it was finished when in death, He commended His spirit into the hands of His Father.

He believed He had achieved that for which He had been born. The questions are, "Did He in fact achieve what He said He did?" and if so, "How can we know?"

Suppose I say to you, "Don't worry about you sins. I'll die for you." So saying, I pull out a revolver, blow my brains out, and there you are surrounded by the mess. Are you any better off than you were before? Has it achieved anything? If not, then what is the significant difference between what I have suggested and that which Jesus did? Can we know for certain that there really is any difference?

Right from the very beginning God said that mankind's rebellion against Him would result in death. In the garden of Eden story God placed a restriction on eating the fruit from the tree of the knowledge of good and evil and fixed a penalty to it: "When you eat of it you will surely die" (Genesis 2:17). This idea is repeated consistently through the Bible. "The wages of sin is death" (Romans 6:23). So the inevitable result of rebellion against God is death.

The penalty — death
The Bible speaks about death in at least three different ways.

(a) *Spiritual death* is a term used to describe the relationship between rebellious mankind and a holy God. So far as our friendship with God is concerned we are dead, life-*less* and we need to be brought back to life. (Ephesians 2:1).

During my life time I have met two people who, because of their actions, were totally disowned by their families. To show how serious this matter was, each family had a funeral notice placed in the newspaper inviting their friends to mourn the death of a son in one case, and a daughter in the other. They would react towards their children from now on as if they were dead. It is rather like that now with us before we come back to God. Not that God disowns us but while we are physically alive, we are dead in our ability and desire to have friendship with God. That is why Jesus says that ". . .unless a man is born again, he cannot see the kingdom of God" (John 3:3). Left to our own desires we cannot change ourselves. We need a miracle to take place.

(b)   *Physical death* is the most natural way to think about death. The Bible takes the view that it also is a result of our rebellion against God. The smashing of well-worked relationships by death with the accompanying pain and sorrow speak to us of a world which is staggering 'out of joint'. Physical death is the symbol of the real death, spiritual death.

(c)   *Eternal death* is also spoken of in the Bible. It can best be described as a state of spiritual death which through our continual rebellion becomes permanent at physical death. This causes us to be in hell, totally separated from God. A death beyond death (John 3:16; Revelation 20:14).

Jesus' death conquers death

Death in every aspect is seen as the result of sin. One follows the other, as night follows day. Well what has this to do with Jesus coming back from death to life? Just this — death follows as the consequence of sin. If Jesus did deal properly with sin in His death then what should we expect to see? Why, the opposite to death — 'up death' — resurrection.

The evidence for the fact that Jesus came back again from the dead is dealt with in chapter seven of this book, however I want to make a distinction between resurrection, resuscitation and re-incarnation.

Christians believe that Jesus was truly dead and that He came back to life again. Not as a ghost or a spirit, but

in the recognisable body He had before. This is what is
meant by resurrection. If you had been there at Palestine
in the first century you could have seen the dead body
placed in the tomb. Three days later you could have seen
Jesus alive and have seen the empty tomb. Some have
suggested that He was not really dead and in the cool of
the tomb He revived and that He was resuscitated and
only appeared to come to life again. Others believe that
Jesus did die but His spirit went on in another body, a
reincarnation. According to this view the original body
decayed away. The eye witnesses reject both these views.
They saw Jesus dead. They saw Him alive again. They
witnessed the empty tomb. They saw this resurrection of
Jesus to be crucial to their understanding of Jesus' work,
and that is how they described it in the Gospels.

In fact, the apostle Paul went so far as to say that if
Jesus is not resurrected from the dead, we can be sure
that His sinbearing death did not 'work', and we are of
all people most miserable because we are still in our sins
and will have to take the punishment ourselves (1 Corinthians 15:17). Nothing significant happened in Jesus'
death if He did not rise from the dead. But He did.

Can we be sure?

From the resurrection of Jesus onwards we can be certain
that the death which Jesus died was a true death which
can deal with the sins of the whole world (1 John 2:2).
That is why it is the cause of endless rejoicing to the
Christian. So important was this event to the first Christians, that they decided to meet together on the first day
of the week as a reminder of Jesus' resurrection since He
rose on that day. There can be no doubt that the death
of Jesus achieved exactly what Jesus said it would. Everything has been done for us to come back, to be forgiven
and to start a new friendship with God.

The death and resurrection of Jesus are seen in the
Bible as one event rather than two. Sometimes the Bible
takes the view that we can be justified before God be-

cause of the *death* of Jesus (Romans 3:24-25) and sometimes because of His *resurrection*. "He was delivered over
to death for our sins and was raised to life for our justification" (Romans 4:25) is the way Paul describes it.

Jesus' resurrection and ours

Another aspect of this great event in the life of Jesus is
described by Paul. He tells us that Jesus' resurrection was
the forerunner to the resurrection of all Christian people. Just as Jesus rose from the dead, then one day they
too will rise with resurrection bodies. You can read this
for yourself in Paul's first letter to the Corinthians (1
Corinthians 15). No doubt he knew this from the words
of Jesus Himself, "Do not be amazed at this, for a time
is coming when all who are in their graves will hear his
voice and come out — those who have done good will
rise to live, and those who have done evil will rise to be
condemned" (John 5:28,29).

Certain about life after death

Since Jesus came back to life again we can be sure that
there really is life after death. This talk of 'pie-in-the-sky-
when-you-die' may have more to it than we thought. It
isn't a total picture of Christianity but we are convinced
that life is more than here and now. There really is a
there and then.

Once at a small discussion group in the home of a
friend, we were talking about the possibilities of life after
death. Imagine my surprise when someone said, "Well
no one has ever come back from the dead to tell us, have
they?" I was not able to restrain myself. "Only one," I
said, "but it only needs one to break the record." I am
old enough to remember when the four minute mile had
not been broken. I well remember the news reaching us
that Roger Bannister of Great Britain had done it. Even
to this day I have never personally witnessed anyone
breaking the four minute mile. But it has never occurred
to me to doubt the historical evidence that it has taken

place. I'm the same about the death and resurrection of
Jesus.

Certain about eternal life

Several conclusions can be drawn about the death and
resurrection of Jesus. Since Jesus has conquered death
He is able to grant eternal life to whom He will. Such, is
His to give. To be separated from Jesus is to remain in
death (John 3:36).

Jesus — Ruler in God's world

Since Jesus' death and resurrection, He has been designated the ruler in God's world. Jesus describes it as, "All
authority in heaven and on earth has been given to me"
(Matthew 28:18). This is especially significant since this
is exactly the way Jesus describes God the Father (Matthew 11:25). "I praise you, Father, Lord of heaven and
earth." The apostle Paul speaks of Jesus in these terms,
". . . he humbled himself and became obedient to death
— even death on a cross. Therefore God exalted him to
the highest place and gave him the name that is above
every name, that at the name of Jesus every knee should
bow, in heaven and on earth and under the earth, and
every tongue confess that Jesus Christ is Lord, to the
glory of God the Father" (Philippians 2:8-11). This is
exactly the way God describes Himself (Isaiah 45:23,24).

It is because of this that the Bible writers warn us of
continued rebellion against the rule of Jesus. We are in
a 'no-win' situation if we continue to oppose Him. Jesus
Himself will be our judge on the day of reckoning. Paul
explained it like this, ". . .he [God] commands all people
everywhere to repent. For he has set a day when he will
judge the world with justice by the man he has appointed.
He has given proof of this to all men by raising him from
the dead" (Acts 17:30,31).

Satan beaten

The last aspect of the death and resurrection of Jesus to which I wish to draw attention is that of the defeat of Satan. Paul, in a letter to the Colossians describes the death of Jesus and its effect in these terms, ". . .and having disarmed the powers and authorities, he made a public spectacle of them, triumphing over them by the cross" (Colossians 2:15). It is a fascinating illustration. When victorious generals came home to Rome they were often given triumphs. Riding at the end of the procession of their victorious troops, the general dragged along behind his chariot the kings and rulers of the country and cities he had conquered. It said in the most graphic way to even the smallest child in Rome, "So great is the power and might of Rome that we turn the rulers of our enemies into our slaves."

Paul picks up the idea and says, 'Do you see the significance of the death and resurrection of Jesus? It is like a triumphant procession in which Jesus demonstrates that He has overpowered all the powers of evil'. It's really great news. No wonder the angels announced it as such to the shepherds when Jesus was born.

He is a wonderful rescuer. He is able to rescue us from the bondage to ourselves, to our sins and to Satan himself.

4.   WHAT IS JESUS DOING NOW?

Luke, in the Book of the Acts of the Apostles, tells us that Jesus appeared regularly over a forty day period following his death and resurrection. Jesus gave clear proof of His resurrection to his followers, so they could be certain beyond doubt, that it had happened. Luke also tells us that Jesus continued to instruct them about the kingdom of heaven (Acts 1:3). On one of these occasions Jesus said to them "Do not leave Jerusalem, but wait for the gift my Father promised, which you have heard me speak about. For John baptised with water, but in a few days you will be baptised with the Holy Spirit" (Acts 1:4,5).

Earlier, at the Last Supper, Jesus instructed the apostles about this important event. He explained to them that He would leave them. They were distressed but Jesus assured them that, although He would not be with them physically, He would come to them through His Holy Spirit and by this means would remain with them permanently.

It is to our advantage that friendship with God is not confined to a fixed physical place, but can be experienced by Christians anywhere and at any time through the Holy Spirit who comes to God's people and remains with them permanently. Jesus explained to the apostles that it was better for them that He should go away so that the Holy Spirit could come to them. While He remained with them, fellowship with Him would be restricted geographically, but after his departure the Spirit Himself would come, and fellowship with God would be unrestricted (see John 14:15-31, 15:26,27, 16:5-15). This coming of the Holy Spirit therefore took place after Jesus returned to heaven where He now reigns as ruler over the creation.

The Holy Spirit, who is also called the Spirit of Jesus Christ (Philippians 1:19), does several things for God's people. He convinces us that our rebellion is serious and that we need forgiveness (John 16:5-15). He is the one who brings us to new birth (John 3:8) and effects a permanent change in us so that we want to please God rather than fight Him (Romans 8:8). He is the one who causes us to become friends with God in the very closest way possible (Romans 8:15,16). He teaches us how to develop that friendship through prayer (Romans 8:26,27) and as we read the Bible. It is He who changes us gradually into people just like Jesus (2 Corinthians 3:18). If He hasn't done this to you yet, you should ask Jesus to send His Holy Spirit to you to bring you back into friendship with God and effect this permanent change. You can be sure that the prayer will be answered. Jesus has promised,

". . . whoever comes to me I will never drive away" (John 6:37).

There is a second aspect to Jesus' present work. The Bible says that in heaven Jesus acts as an intercessor for His people (Hebrews 6:17-20; 7:25; 1 John 2:1,2). He is praying for us. Everything about Jesus' life and work gives us confidence to know that God has never for a moment lost interest in His world or the people in it.

5. WHY IS JESUS RETURNING AGAIN?

At the moment that Jesus returned to heaven, Luke tells us that two men dressed in white (angels?) stood by the disciples and said, "Men of Galilee, why do you stand here looking into the sky? This same Jesus, who has been taken from you into heaven, will come back in the same way you have seen him go into heaven" (Acts 1:11). The New Testament writers agree that the present world order will not go on indefinitely. The birth-life-death cycle with which we are familiar will have an end. The history of this world is not endless. The God who lifted the blind on our history when He said "Let there be light" (Genesis 1:3) is the same God who will pull down the blind on history by the return to earth again of Jesus.

The reign of Jesus is real. Made fact by His death and resurrection, it is only recognised by His people. Jesus will end creation's history by His return and will demonstrate to all the world that He is indeed King in God's world. He will do that by judging us all. In his speech at Athens, Paul described the event in this way:

". . . he [God] commands all people everywhere to repent. For he has set a day when he will judge the world with justice by the man he has appointed. He has given proof of this to all men by raising him from the dead" (Acts 17:30,31).

What Paul said was consistent with the teaching of Jesus about His return in Matthew 24:26-51; 25:31-46; John 5:24-29. While the descriptions of Jesus' return, or second coming, do not tell how or when the event will happen, they leave no doubt that it will take place, and several things are very clear.

Jesus will return.

He will return in triumph and power.

He will judge the living and the dead.

His judgement will be executed impartially on the basis of justice and truth.

He will set up a new heaven and a new earth in which righteousness will dwell and all evil will be abolished.

Justice and right do not always prevail in this present world. Our world cries out for justice. It cannot possibly be right that a Hitler who commits suicide could be the same as a poor disturbed person who ends his life in loneliness and despair, unable to work out the answer to his present problems.

I know of a young mother who has three sons, two not yet at school. The mother has leukaemia, and everything in me cries out, "It's not fair. What has she done? Is she any worse than I am? Here am I, fit and well and she is dying. I am unmarried without dependents, she has a husband and three small children." *It isn't fair.*

You see how evil sinning is. Look at the mess it has got us into. It would have been much easier if we had never turned away from God. Sinning is so evil that its effects *are* unfair and indiscriminate. Justice is not in this world, but that does not mean that there is no eventual justice. Jesus will return and judge the world impartially and according to truth. In this world it is often difficult to apportion blame correctly. In the day of judgement all wrong will be seen for what it is, as all good will also be seen for what it is. There will be no confusion, right will triumph over wrong. No doubt that is why the Psalmist is able to rejoice at the prospect: "Sing to the Lord a new song. . . Shout for joy to the Lord, all the earth, burst into jubilant song with music; . . . for he comes to judge the earth. He will judge the world in righteousness and the peoples with equity" (Psalm 98:1,4,8,9).

When that happens, God's people will live in a new creation where there will be no more death, pain, tears. It is described poetically as a place where the wolf and the lamb will feed together; the lion will eat straw with the ox, (which is good news for the lamb and the ox); and where the child will play at the hole of the cobra and where nothing will be hurt nor destroy (Isaiah 11:8; 65:25). In fact, it will be like being back in a Garden of Eden situation. People in harmony with God, in harmony with each other, and in harmony with their environment.

So good will it be, that we can be excused for asking the question, "If all wrong is to be abolished, and justice is to prevail, then why hasn't Jesus come back?" In our best moments we say, "The world is in such a mess, how can God stand it? Why doesn't He do something?"

One thing is certain. He is no less caring than we are, nor is He less interested in the world, nor is He less loving than we are. In fact, it is the exact opposite. It is because He loves the world and the people in it that He delays his return. Peter explains why: "The Lord is not slow in keeping his promise, as some understand slowness. He is patient with you, not wanting anyone to perish, but everyone to come to repentance" (2 Peter 3:9).

God has made us people with a will. We are responsible people. God has shown His love to us and He desires us to exercise our wills and love Him. He will not take our wills away or make us less than true people. He seeks to convince us. He calls on us to return to Him. Sometimes in words of command (Acts 17:30). Sometimes with gentle invitation (Matthew 11:28). Sometimes with persistent knocking (Revelation 3:20), but we can be sure He will not force Himself into our lives. You can't *make* people love you.

When I was a child my father would sometimes say, "Don't do that, John." He might even repeat it, "Didn't I tell you, John, don't do that." Sometimes he would extend the moment of his judgment, "John, I've told you a dozen times not to do that!" What causes that behaviour? Is it just because he was a weak man? Surely not. It was because he longed for me to voluntarily return his love in obedience. He did not take any pleasure in punishing me. So he extended the 'judgment'. Sometimes I came good; sometimes I got what I deserved. God does exactly that. He extends the time so that we will repent. He warns us that it will not be like this forever but while there is still time, we can turn back and return His love. I have always considered myself to be a very fortunate man that God's judgment day has been delayed long enough for me to turn back and stop rebelling.

Can I say to you, don't push your luck too far. It might be today.

CHAPTER FIVE

What's it Like to be a Christian?

Up to now we have looked at the world as it is and ourselves as we are. We have set out, all of us, in one way or another to try and relate to God in a way which we know is unsatisfactory. We have either ignored Him or tried to use Him or else simply rebelled in open hostility. God has responded in an unexpected way. He has sent Jesus, His only Son, into the world to show us what He is like so that we can enter into friendship with Him. He has allowed Him to die so that friendship can be possible without sacrificing His purity or His goodness. He calls us to take stock of our position and to turn away from independence and become friends again.

In all meaningful relationships, commitment is involved. We commit ourselves to the other party and they to us. It is like that in a true friendship with God. Jesus commits Himself to us and we to Him. So that we can fully understand what is involved I will look at both these aspects.

1. JESUS' COMMITMENT TO HIS PEOPLE — NOW

What does it really mean to have Jesus commit Himself to us? He describes this relationship with an illustration of a shepherd with his sheep.

". . . the sheep listen to his (the shepherd's) voice. He calls his own sheep by name and leads them out. When he has brought out all his own, he goes on ahead of them, and his sheep follow him because they know his voice. . . I have come that they may have life and have it to the full. I am the good shepherd. The good shepherd lays down his life for the sheep" (John 10:3-11).

Until I became a school teacher, I had always lived in the city of Sydney. I knew very little about farm life and nothing about grazing. My first teaching appointment was in northern New South Wales in some of the finest wheat farming and sheep grazing country in Australia. My education began all over again. Sheep farming in this country is very different from that described in the Bible by Jesus. I saw a flock of sheep larger than a thousand being driven from behind with a couple of drovers and some very well trained sheep dogs. The dogs buzzed around barking, and by a not too gentle nip on the ankles, persuading any reluctant sheep to obey them. In fact the place where I lived had a couple of sheep dogs who were too old to work and had been brought in from the property to 'retire'. They often kept in practice by rounding up the chickens and ducks. Any egg that was laid there, was laid 'on the run'.

The picture which Jesus gives us of sheep grazing in the first century Palestine is very different and also very appealing. The flock was small. Each sheep was known personally and by name. The shepherd went in front as a guide. He led them to where they could pasture. He protected them with his life. It is a perfect picture of Jesus with His people.

Because of Jesus we are significant — now

When Jesus commits Himself to us it is personal and individual. Such is the nature of the relationship between Jesus and His people that He comes and lives permanently with every one. He does this through His Holy Spirit (John 14:23). So far as Jesus is concerned we are not just one tiny speck among hundreds of millions of tiny specks on some distant planet. God is not to be thought of as being too busy attending to more important things than to be worried about us. God is to be thought of as a shepherd who knows each one *by name* and who calls each one *by name*. I don't know if you think you are a significant person or not. God thinks you are. So much so that He calls you into a friendship with Him, person to person.

Matthew closes his Gospel with these very reassuring words of Jesus, "Surely I will be with you always, to the very end of the age" (Matthew 28:20). One of the great benefits of a true friendship with Jesus is the experience of knowing that I am cared for, loved, and known 'by name'. There is no situation in life where I am completely alone. Often I find I am misunderstood by people — sometimes even by my family and friends. It is reassuring to know that I am never misunderstood or ignored by Jesus.

Because of Jesus we are secure — now

When Jesus commits Himself to us as a Shepherd, He also becomes a guide through life. The picture is of Jesus in front leading the way. This is exactly what He meant when He said,

"I am the light of the world. Whoever follows me will never walk in darkness, but will have the light of life" (John 8:12).

A young salesman came into our office selling stationery and we got into conversation over coffee. He said he'd had many jobs over the last five years and I asked him if he was satisfied with life and if he knew what life was about. In a moment of disarming honesty he said, "I don't know what life is about and I don't know where I'm heading." I think it was only then that I fully realised that it is Jesus who gives life its meaning and direction.

I don't know if you have ever asked yourself the really great questions of life. Who am I? What am I doing here? Where am I going? What is life about? I think it's very difficult to arrive at any satisfactory answers to them without Jesus. He says, "I am the way, and the truth and the life" (John 14:6). At rock bottom, life is about being in relationship with Jesus and growing like Him.

Because of Jesus we can be forgiven — now

He is the good shepherd who lays down His life for His sheep. There is nothing that He will not do for the protection of His people. He has died so that our sin can be forgiven and that the guilty conscience can be dealt with. All of us have done things in the past which we regret or wish had been otherwise. Sometime our past rises up and accuses us. Some people's memory of their past has been such that it affects them mentally and physically to the present.

Specialist counsellors, doctors and clergymen are being called upon by an increasing number of people needing treatment for emotional guilt. Very often, the guilt manifests itself in real physical symptoms or disabilities. In one instance of which I know, a colleague was called upon to counsel at length a lady who was in such great mental distress that her health was seriously affected. Even though she had asked my colleague for help, for a very long time she was still unable to tell him what was really troubling her. Eventually however, she told him of something which had happened over thirty years before, when she was a young teenager and which she had never been able to speak about to anyone. This experience from her past haunted her, she felt guilty and unforgiven, and the past had assumed more importance and reality than the present.

You may be like that woman. Whether you are or not, your conscience is marred, you feel guilty and unforgiven, but in a true friendship with Jesus your past has been forgiven and forgotten. You are treated as if you had never sinned.

Many years ago I was speaking on this subject at the University of New England. In the group was a young man who had come to us from one of the top Grammar Schools. He was a most impressive man, bursting with potential and leadership ability. He said, "Are you actually saying that God will forget completely about my past?" I replied that it was exactly what I was saying. His eyes filled with tears as he declared, "That's almost too good to be true."

And I agreed with him. I knew nothing about his past life, any more than I know about yours, but I do know that God's forgiveness through Jesus, is "almost too good to be true" for any of us.

Because of Jesus we can have eternal life — now

Eternal life is an interesting concept. When the Bible uses it, it does so to denote a God-quality of life which, because it is His, goes on forever. The idea that life would just go on and on forever is a fairly daunting one if you don't have any prospect that it will get better.

When Jesus says, "I have come that you might have life and have it to the full' (John 10:10) He is referring to a quality of life which comes from friendship with God. Jesus Himself begins to transform us permanently into new people by His Holy Spirit. Eternal life is not something which happens when you die. John tells us that "God so loved the world that he gave his one and only Son, that whoever believes in him shall not perish, but have [right now] eternal life" (John 3:16).

To the woman at the well Jesus said, "Everyone who drinks this water will be thirsty again, but whoever drinks the water I give him will never thirst. Indeed, the water I give him will become in him a spring of water welling up to eternal life" (John 4:13,14).

Jesus brings the endless search to an end and satisfies the deep longings of the soul. He gives life meaning and direction.

Because of Jesus we can have a new life — now

When, before His death, Jesus explained to His disciples that He would go away, He also promised that they would not be left alone, for He would send His Spirit to come and live with them (John 16:6,7). The Holy Spirit is sometimes referred to in the Bible as the "Spirit of Jesus" (Philippians 1:19), the "Holy Spirit" (Luke 11:13), or just the "Spirit" (Philippians 2:1). His work is to make us into new people. So great is the change which He makes, that a person who has been given the Holy Spirit by Jesus is said to be 'born again'. Peter describes it like this, "Praise be to the God and Father of our Lord Jesus Christ! In his great mercy he has given us new birth into a living hope through the resurrection of Jesus Christ from the dead" (1 Peter 1:3).

The Spirit gives us a desire to grow like Jesus and a new potential to face life. He transforms us. When I was in theological college an evangelist visited us. He told us that as a child he was frightened of his father who drank excessively and when drunk used to beat the family. He had sold the furniture from their home to satisfy this habit and often the family went without food. One night the man stopped and listened to a Salvation Army open-air meeting. He heard about Jesus and what He had done. The man turned back to Jesus and asked Him to forgive him and make him into a new person. This took place. He still had the same problems — the family was still frightened of him — the home still had no furniture but now he had a new potential to face them. The family was sceptical as to whether any real change had taken place. But each night he came home sober. On the next Friday night he arrived home with a full pay packet. First time in anyone's memory. That week they all ate. The next week he came home with a chair and they all played games by sitting on it in turn. As the months went by the whole family began to come back to some degree of normality. The change took place in the father in a moment of time. It took years for that change to work itself out in practice. The Holy Spirit gives a new potential to help us face life and live it properly.

I was working in the follow-up section of a Billy Graham Crusade in 1979, helping people who had become Christians, and I heard a remarkable story about a married couple who had been converted. The marriage was not good and they had finally parted. Unknown to each other, each had gone to the Crusade and they had both been converted. After the Crusade, the man decided he should contact his wife and so he phoned her to ask if he could come and see her that night. She was wary and said that she had made arrangements to go out, but he persisted saying, "It really is very important. Where are you planning to go anyway?"

"Well, if you must know I'm going to a Bible study." He was stunned and rushed to explain what had happened to him at the Crusade. A couple of days later they met, talked and in a few months, with help from others, they got back together again. They still had problems but they had a new potential with which to face them.

What the Holy Spirit does. The result of the work of the Holy Spirit is described like this:

"The fruit of the Spirit is love, joy, peace, patience, kindness, goodness, faithfulness, gentleness and self control" (Galatians 5:22,23).

The Holy Spirit begins to work in our lives and can cause all those God-like attributes to grow and develop in each of His people.

Because of Jesus we need have no fear of death — now

In the western world, at the present moment, we have a strange fear of death. We pretend it will never happen, at least to us. We hardly ever speak about it. We sometimes do in the abstract but hardly ever do we talk about our own death. When we do, people say we are morbid. Our fear of death can be seen in the great lengths to which we go to pretend we are younger than we are. With death all around us we have a strange indisposition to face our own.

In His famous statement made at the time when He raised His friend Lazarus from the dead, Jesus declares

"I am the resurrection and the life. He who believes in me will live, even though he dies; and whoever lives and believes in me will never die" (John 11:26).

Death has no terror for the child of God. He knows that he will be secure with Jesus, the Lord of life, death and life after death.

I draw a distinction between death and the process of dying. No one could look forward to dying although it may be worse for those of us who watch it than those who undergo it. But there is no fear of death or its results for the child of God.

Because of Jesus we can be part of a new family — now

On one occasion when Jesus was teaching a crowd of people, His mother and His brothers arrived. They were outside the house where Jesus was and sent a message to Him. Someone in the crowd said, "Your mother and brothers are outside looking for you."

"Who are my mother and my brothers?" He asked.

Then He looked at those seated in a circle around Him and said, "Here are my mother and my brothers. Whoever does God's will is my brother and sister and mother" (Mark 3:32-35).

Not only will Jesus make us new people but He promises to put us into a new family with His people. To be united to Jesus is to be united with those who are His — the Church.

Some people have had bad experiences with the church but that has not been my experience. I have found that they are kind, thoughtful and forgiving. Whenever I have travelled the world over, be it in Australia or in the UK, USA, Canada, the Continent, Africa, India, Singapore, Hong Kong, Papua New Guinea or Pakistan, and I have found Christ's people, I have been received as family. On some occasions I was only just able to make myself understood, so little of their language had I; but I was always received with love.

Not only is it a new family but it is large and its members come from such diverse backgrounds. There is no doubt in my mind that had I not been a Christian I would never have met the wide circle of friends which I have made. I will describe my own church later in chapter 14, but I did not want to wait to point out this aspect of Christ's commitment to us.

Because of Jesus our prayers can be heard — now
A colleague of mine tells a story about going to a new barber in his suburb. The barber asked if he lived in the district and he said he did. "I haven't seen you at the local pub," said the barber.

"No," was the reply, "I don't go there."

"Where do you drink?" he persisted.

"As a matter of fact I don't drink beer at all."

"Well then, how do you cope with your problems?"

"Lots of ways. I talk about them with my wife, sometimes with my friends, but really I pray about my problems."

Like my colleague, I don't need to find an artificial or temporary relief from problems. I can face them with the sure knowledge that I am not on my own; although I don't have a partner or family with which to share, I am assured that Jesus does hear my prayers.

We can all have that certain knowledge that Jesus will hear and answer our prayers if we are in right relationship with Him. He has promised that He will hear us when we ask, and will answer our requests in the way *which is best for us.* That may not always be the way we think our prayers should be answered, but God will always act towards us like a loving, responsible Father. Every request will be heard, and will be answered in a way which will help us most.

Just before His death, Jesus said to His disciples,

"And I will do whatever you ask in my name, so that the Son may bring glory to the Father. You may ask me for anything in my name, and I will do it" (John 14:13,14).

The phrase "in my name" means "according to my character".

To have Jesus commit Himself to us is a great privilege indeed. His pledge is to make us significant and secure, to forgive us and give us eternal life. He promises to give us a new life through His spirit living with us. He places us in a new family, takes the fear out of death and promises to hear our prayers. It may sound too good to be true but it is the experience of all Christian people.

However the relationship is not one sided. He commits Himself to us. What is the nature of our commitment to Him? Jesus tells us exactly under what conditions He will be our friend.

2. OUR COMMITMENT TO JESUS — NOW

Jesus said "If anyone would come after me, he must deny himself and take up his cross daily and follow me. For whoever wants to save his life will lose it, but whoever loses his life for me will save it. What good is it for a man to gain the whole world and yet lose or forfeit his very self?" (Luke 9:23-25).

When Jesus spoke about "taking up the cross", He was speaking about giving up the claim to our lives. It meant being prepared for execution. No one who heard Jesus could have mistaken His meaning. They knew what crucifixion was.

In the year 6 A.D., when Jesus was about twelve years old, a Galilean named Judas led a major Jewish uprising against the Romans who had recently occupied Judaea. The rebellion was crushed and the surviving rebels were almost certainly crucified. It is likely that the boy Jesus and his contemporaries would have witnessed the horrors of crucifixion, since the Romans usually executed their victims along roadsides and in prominent places. The message was to be clear to all: 'Do not resist Roman might'.

No doubt it made a vivid impression on the mind of the young man, Jesus. Everyone knew what He meant. If we are to maintain friendship with the Lord Jesus, then we are to daily surrender our wills and minds to Him, which always seems more difficult to do when you're on the outside looking in than it does from the inside looking out. Surrender it is, but it is surrender into friendship, into life itself. To stay independent is to "lose life" even though we were to gain the whole world, which is a substantial prize! To surrender my independence is to gain "life to the full" (John 10:10).

Let me tell you about a young couple, Tom and Sally, who have just fallen in love. He is completely gone, head over heels. Tom's relationship to Sally can be described in various ways depending on your outlook. If you are talking to Tom's friends they will describe his new behaviour like this, "We don't know what's got into him lately. We think he's gone off his rocker. He doesn't chat up the birds anymore. He doesn't drink with the blokes on Friday nights. Someone told me that he went to the Art Gallery last Sunday! Imagine Tom at an art gallery. I hope they've got those paintings insured. What's more, someone said that he has sold his surf board, although I can't believe that."

On the other hand Tom's description will run like this, "I've met this wonderful girl, Sally. She's so fascinating that I can't stop thinking about her. We've been going to all sorts of places together and she has got some marvellous friends."

If I were to say to him, "But you've made some fairly big sacrifices to enter into this friendship, haven't you?" He would be amazed. "You don't drink with the blokes on Fridays. You don't chat up the birds any more. Is it a fact you've sold your surf board? They are fairly hefty sacrifices, aren't they?"

"Sacrifices? Don't be silly, I just can't do those things and be with Sally. It's as simple as that."

In all friendships it depends on whether you're on the outside looking in or on the inside looking out.

It is possible to describe Christianity as a long list of activities you are not allowed to do. On the other hand it should be rightly thought of in terms of the person of the Lord Jesus and the positive changes that He will bring.

Earlier, I described my encounter with the history lecturer and made the point that we need to defer to those who have special knowledge which we don't possess. If we pretend to know better than they do, when it is obvious that we don't, then there is not much future for that friendship. We need to surrender our wills to Jesus, because of the comprehensive nature of His special knowledge.

John opens his Gospel with a description of Jesus whom he describes as a specialist in at least four areas:
1 Knowledge of God
2 Creativity
3 Living
4 Morality

> John says, "In the beginning was the Word [Jesus], and the Word was with God and the Word was God. He was with God in the beginning. Through him all things were made; without him nothing was made that has been made. In him was life, and that life was the light of men. The light shines in the darkness, but the darkness has not overcome it" (John 1:1-5).

1. Jesus is a specialist in knowing God.
"The Word was with God and the Word was God". There is no reason why I shouldn't have a really good friendship with Jesus as long as I don't become a bore and start correcting His theology.

If I want to find out about you, the persons to ask are those who live with you. The longer you've been living with them, the better the extent of their knowledge. John tells us of Jesus (the Word), that He has been with the Father from all eternity. There is no one who is better qualified to tell us about God. He has been with Him all the time. So when Jesus tells us what God is like, which is theology, then the Christian believes it. He may have to modify some of his earlier views. He may have to abandon some, and others will be confirmed. But it is impossible for me to enter into relationship with Jesus and then to start correcting His theology. He is a specialist in theology. When Jesus says, "I am the way, and the truth and the life. No one comes to the Father except through me" (John 14:6), then Christian, believe it.

Jesus knows how God acts and feels. He is privy to the plans of God. We are constantly wanting to remake God in our own image. We want to be able to contain Him. I wrote this book during a Christmas break. I was at church on Christmas Day and wondered why there were so many people there who normally didn't come. Is it that while we think about Jesus as the baby in the stable He is so helpless that He makes no demands on us at all. We are able to contain 'the baby'. But the Word who was with God and who *is* God and who has always been, is a different matter altogether. He, and He alone, is able to say what God is like.

2. Jesus is a specialist in creativity

"All things were created by Him". When the Sydney Opera House was opened we had a marvellous series of concerts to celebrate the event. I was able to go to only one of them. Lorin Maazell conducted the Cleveland Orchestra and Birgit Nilsson sang. I had heard her recordings and admired her tremendously. The first part of the concert was great, although Birgit Nilsson was scheduled to sing only in the second half, so after the interval I settled back to enjoy that part for which I had come. The orchestra struck up, and began to play so loudly I was stunned. "I've really wasted my money" I thought. I'll never hear

her above that!" I was mistaken. Suddenly a voice rang out. It was as loud as a cannon and as clear as a bell, and there followed fifteen minutes of the most superb music-making it has been my pleasure to have experienced. At the conclusion I didn't have enough limbs to stamp and clap. It was a truly brilliant moment. But reflect what went into that moment of pleasure. To start with there was the genius of the composer who wrote the music. There was the hard work and skill of a lifetime of practice and experience which Birgit Nilsson brought with her creativity. The same could be said of Lorin Maazell and the seventy or so members of the orchestra. There was a great deal of creativity in that marvellous moment. It was moving to reflect that Jesus was the creator of all creativity — "Without him nothing was made that has been made."

I have on my wall a print of Frank McCubbin's, *The Child Lost*. The original is in the Victorian Arts Centre in Melbourne. When I look at it, it evokes in me all the feeling I have for the Australian bush land. I feel as though I can smell the eucalypts and I want to pack up and go bush-walking immediately. How can a painter do that?

Once again that might not be your scene but at some time you must have been staggered by some moments of great creativity when your mouth dropped open and you said, "What a genius! How can anyone do that?" Jesus is a specialist in creativity. More and more I am learning to appreciate this marvellous world which the Master Creator provides for me to live in. Yet unlike all others, Jesus does His creating from nothing. He brings into being things which never existed before. Our own creativity is always dependent upon what already is.

When I was on the outside of Christianity looking in, my great fear was that if I surrendered myself to Jesus, I would lose all individuality and creativity. I thought it would be a dreary life in the 'greys'. I don't know why I thought that, but I was completely inaccurate. Jesus is a specialist in creativity.

Understanding this aspect will help us from falling into two real errors in life. Some people do not recognise Jesus as creator, worship the world, use it completely for their own pleasure and neglect the giver. Others, not realising that the creation was given to us to enjoy, become ascetics and cut themselves off from the world. Christians enjoy the creation knowing who made it and why.

3. Jesus is a specialist in living

"In Him was life". Jesus is not so far off, that He neither knows nor cares about us in the life situation. He has been where we are and where we have been. He has lived life with its joys and sorrows. He knows what living is like. But best of all He knows what it is about. He tells me which things in life are important and which are trivial. So when He says that I am to seek the kingdom of God first and not spend my life acquiring possessions or hoarding things (Matthew 6:33), I am slowly learning to believe and do as He says. He is a specialist in life.

4. Jesus is a specialist in morality

"The darkness has not overcome it". He is to say what is right and what is wrong. He is light and in Him is no darkness at all (1 John 1:5). We live at a time in which we have been taught to think that morality is relative and personal. So we say, "That's wrong for you but it's all right for me." A true friendship with Jesus will mean a modification of my views on morality. What Jesus says is right. He is a specialist in morality.

Earlier in this book I described a visit I made with a friend, Tim, to the National Gallery in London. He took me around the seventeenth century paintings. I made the point that when we defer to those who know more than we do the result is always life-expanding.

Because of Jesus' comprehensive expertise, to defer to

Him is life-expanding in every direction. He gives us a new outlook towards other people, money and property, our enemies, those in need, acts of kindness, worry and true wisdom. You can read about them in His great Sermon on the Mount (Matthew chapters 5 to 7).

What is to be done?

Up to now I have tried to show the Bible's analysis of our present problem and God's solution in Jesus Christ.

Depending on where you are at right now, there are three different ways of proceeding with this book.

1. I have shown how Jesus promises to commit Himself to us and how we are to commit ourselves to Him. You may be ready to do that now. If so, my suggestion would be that you skip the next two sections of this book and proceed immediately to Section 4: *"What Am I Supposed To Do?"*.

2. You may, however, find that you have basically agreed with what has been said so far but you don't want to commit yourself to Christ yet. May I suggest that you proceed to Section 3: *"What's The Alternative?"*.

3. On the other hand you may find yourself unable to commit yourself to Christ because you are uncertain about whether God really does exist. My suggestion is that you continue to Section 2: *"Can We Really Know?"*. I have set out there why I believe that God *is*, that Jesus is God's unique Son and that the Bible gives us reliable information about God and ourselves.

Part 2

Can We Really Know?

CHAPTER SIX

Will the True God Please Stand Up

"*What does God mean to you? Do you believe in Him in the biblical sense, or does He exist in a different way?*"

Bob Hawke former Australian Labor Party spokesman for industrial relations [Prime Minister from 1983]:

"Being an agnostic, how does one answer the question, 'What does God mean to you?' I am not sure if there is one, a God or not. . ."

Professor Manning Clark, author and historian:

"God means part of the quest to believe. I sometimes believe in God as portrayed by the Bible; the New Testament sometimes and the Old Testament never. . ."

Norm Gallagher, federal secretary of the Builders' Labourers' Union:

"I believe the only thing that is going to save me is the working class. They're my god. I have no religious beliefs whatsoever. I don't believe in God as portrayed in the Bible. I haven't seen him. . . I haven't met him. . ."

Frank Galbally, lawyer:

"To me God means everything. He represents to me the hope and expectations that go far beyond anything which mortal man can achieve without him. . ."

The Weekend Australian
January 9-10, 1982. Page 7.

Collectively these answers present several possible views. Some people are thoroughly convinced about the existence of God, some are uncertain, while others are not convinced at all.

If you are uncertain, let me share with you why I believe in the existence of God.

Only with evidence

If I arrive at a bus stop and discover that there are two people waiting there, I *know* they are there because I can see them, hear them speaking to each other and I suppose I could reach out and touch them. That they are there is beyond reasonable doubt. The evidence is too strong.

In the final chapter of Harper Lee's "To Kill a Mockingbird", there is a description of two children returning home from a party at the school. As they walk through the woods they think they hear footsteps following them. When they stop to listen the footsteps stop. They are terrified. Suddenly with a loud shout, their attacker rushes at them. They suspected someone was there long before they saw him but when he finally attacked, they were certain of his presence. The evidence was over-whelming.

The Bible claims that God had been giving mankind evidence of His existence right from the beginning of the world. And then He came right out in the open in an historical event in the person of Jesus Christ.

Why Jesus?

Suppose you were shipwrecked on a desert island and as you began to explore you came across a garden with carefully planted beds of vegetables and flowers. They were growing well. The plots were weeded and obviously cared for. It would be possible to believe that this had all happened by chance, but it would be more probable to suppose that someone had done it.

If as you explored further you found garden tools, a compost heap and a smouldering incinerator, they would all tend to confirm your view. Finally if the gardener himself stepped out from behind a tree your supposition that someone had done all the work would be confirmed. Then if he took you around his garden and explained why he planned it in such a way and how he accomplished it, you would learn something about the kind of person he was, and the purpose for all he had done.

The Bible takes the view that the world around us speaks about God's existence. It is possible that the creation all happened by chance. That is a fairly long shot. It is more probable that someone caused it. The Bible says that God did it.

God continued to show and tell us of His existence through His people, the Jews, and through the prophets whom He sent to them. Finally God 'stepped out from behind the tree'. He sent His Son, Jesus to become a man so that we could know that He exists and exactly what He is like. The Bible puts it like this:

"In the past God spoke to our forefathers through the prophets at many times and in various ways, but in these last days he has spoken to us by his Son, whom he appointed heir of all things; and through whom he made the universe" (Hebrews 1:1,2).

God has not been hiding. He has been showing mankind that He is there. One of our problems is that we often look in the wrong place. Jesus Christ claimed that He showed us God's character. When one of the disciples said to Him at the Last Supper, "Lord, show us the Father and that will be enough for us," Jesus answered: "Don't you know me, Philip, even after I have been among you such a long time? Anyone who has seen me has seen the Father" (John 14:8,9).

God does not ask for blind faith or a leap in the dark. He provides us with evidence which is beyond doubt so that our faith can rest on the facts. These facts focus on Jesus, so it is to Him we look.

There is no doubt that this man who lived almost 2,000 years ago in Palestine lived a remarkable life, and that

His effect on the history of the world is sufficient to warrant investigation.

Jesus claimed to be the unique Son of God. This and other claims are so outrageous that if they are not true then there was something seriously wrong with Him. However, if they are true then He should be worshipped as God the Son.

We need to look very carefully at this impressive person.

CHAPTER SEVEN

Impressive, Outrageous, but Believable

Some people are impressive because of their quick wit. Sir Robert Menzies, one time Prime Minister of Australia, was heckled by someone in the crowd who said, "Tell us all you know, Bob — it won't take long!" As quick as a flash came the reply — "I'll tell you everything we both know — it won't take any longer!"[1] On another occasion someone said, "I wouldn't vote for you if you were the Archangel Gabriel" to which he replied, "If I were the Archangel Gabriel, madam, I'm afraid you would not be in my constituency."[2]

I read in Kenneth Edward's book "I Wish I'd Said That!" the following: "On the first night of one of his plays Oscar Wilde stood in the foyer of the theatre, receiving bouquets of flowers from his admirers. One member of the audience who was far from being one of his admirers and wished to humiliate him, presented him with a rotten cabbage.

'Thank you, my dear fellow,' said Wilde. 'Everytime I smell it I shall be reminded of you'."[3]

Some people impress us with their physical skills. I once saw the Moscow Circus when they toured this country. The skill of the acrobats was breathtaking. As I watched them I couldn't help asking the question, "How many times have they practised that act so that night after night they can do it and not fall?" Some years later, I

1. *The Wit Of Sir Robert Menzies* Ray Robinson, Outback Press 1978.
2. *Ibid.*
3. *I Wish I'd Said That* Kenneth Edwards, Abelard-Schuman 1976.

thought that the most impressive part of the Moscow Olympics was the near perfection of the gymnasts.

Some people are impressive because of their moral courage. I was teaching in a country town where there were about fifty teachers on the staff of the school. At a meeting of staff, someone suggested a course of action which, to say the least, was ethically doubtful. A young man, fresh from teachers' college and the youngest member of staff, rose to his feet and in a quiet voice, but with enough nervousness to show that he meant it, said, "Headmaster if you do that I will expose you. I will write to the Minister for Education, the Area Director and the newspapers. You must do what you think is right but so must I." He calmly sat down. He was the only person in the room who was calm. However, the matter was dropped and to my knowledge it was never raised again. He was a very impressive young man. The Australian word for it is 'guts'.

Impressive as such people are in one way or another, Jesus Christ puts Himself into a different category altogether. His claims are absolutely outrageous, and if they are not true, then something is definitely wrong with Him. Yet He seems quite believable. Indeed so outrageous are these claims that we are left with only a few options.

C.S. Lewis in *Mere Christianity* puts it this way:

"A man who was merely a man and said the sort of things Jesus said would not be a great moral teacher. He would either be a lunatic — on the level with the man who says he is a poached egg — or else He would be the Devil of Hell. You must make a choice. Either this man was, and is, the Son of God: or else a madman or something worse. You can shut Him up for a fool, you can spit at Him and kill Him as a demon; or you can fall at His feet and call Him Lord and God. But let us not come with any patronising nonsense about

His being a great human teacher. He has not left that open to us. He did not intend to."[1]

Some people have suggested to me that He *is* a good moral teacher and a fine example to follow, yet they baulk at confessing Him as Lord and God. I am convinced that this position cannot be held in the light of the evidence in the gospels. Such are His claims that if He is right then He is *Lord*. If He is wrong then He is totally deluded — a *lunatic* or worse, He is a *liar*.

What do you think about Him?

I have been convinced that the evidence points in only one direction. To show what I mean I will draw your attention to three major aspects of the person of Jesus.

1. HIS OUTRAGEOUS CLAIMS
2. HIS BELIEVABLE ACTIONS.
3. HIS RESURRECTION FROM DEATH

1. HIS OUTRAGEOUS CLAIMS

Space will not permit us to deal with all the claims of Jesus, but I have selected six very different ones.
Jesus claimed to be:
a) The bread of life
b) The light of the world
c) The giver of eternal life
d) The forgiver of sins
e) The judge of the world
f) Lord and God

a) The bread of life

On one occasion while addressing a large crowd, Jesus said: "I am the bread of life. He who comes to me will never go hungry, and he who believes in me will never be thirsty" (John 6:35). It is clear from the rest of the speech that Jesus is claiming to be able to give people satisfaction in life rather than to physically feed them.

1. *Mere Christianity* C.S. Lewis, W.M. Collins Fontana Books 1970.

However, it is a very bold statement. You and I know how difficult it is to find satisfaction in life for ourselves. That is hard enough. It's even more difficult to satisfy all the needs of another. That's really hard work. However, to keep the family satisfied, that's nearly impossible.

In England in 1980, some friends staying near Cambridge decided to come to London for a weekend to see the sights. I wrote and asked them to let me know what they wanted to see so I could plan out the best way to see most. I sent them a tourist guide book of London. After about two weeks I got a reply. It said, "In as much as it is ever possible for the Hawkes family to ever agree on anything, the following seem to be the places we would like to see." I smiled at their honesty.

Don't you think it a very bold statement for a man to make: "Anyone, anywhere, under any set of circumstances, come to me and I will give you life satisfaction." That seems to be the impact of His statement. What is more, the Christians whom I know, all claim that that is exactly what has happened to them.

Although I believe Jesus' statement, I am not necessarily asking you to believe it. What I am saying is that it is outrageous if it is not true.

b) The light of the world

On another occasion Jesus said, "I am the light of the world. Whoever follows me will never walk in darkness, but will have the light of life" (John 8:12). What a statement! You can hardly imagine anyone thinking it, let alone saying it. What would you think if having read this book up to this point you discovered a statement like this: "I'm glad you've read this book because I am the only person who really understands life and now I will tell you exactly and precisely what it is all about. If you follow what I say, you will understand life. If not, you will be mistaken forever. That is how significant my words are."

Surely you would conclude that my case was serious and that I was in need of treatment. Yet that is exactly what Jesus is saying, "I am the light of the world." He is not claiming to be just one more enlightened person amongst many others, but *the* source of all understanding. It isn't as if He claims even to bring new light onto old problems, but what He is claiming is to be *the* light of the world. Jesus' claim is to be able to give life direction to those who follow Him, together with the understanding about the meaning of life. It is a very bold statement with the equally bold implication that if a person does not follow Him, he will remain in the darkness and never understand what life is about.

No wonder the Jewish leaders in Jesus' time reacted as they did to His statement. "Here you are," they said, "appearing as your own witness; your testimony is not valid" (John 8:13). They are saying, "You are all talk. How can you substantiate such a claim?"

Yet Christians whom I know, claim that Jesus has given their lives new meaning and direction. They don't hesitate to agree that His claim is well founded. If I had claimed to be the 'light of the world' that claim would be completely outrageous. No one would take me seriously. When Jesus made the claim it was believable because His words and His actions were all in line with it.

One of the difficulties for us as twentieth century nuclear age people, is that we almost all have a mental picture of Jesus, but very few of us have read the histories about Him. For most He is a shadowy, golden-haired young man who wandered around Palestine in the first century patting little children on the head and saying something like, "Be good for goodness sake because it's good to be good." There is no substitute for reading the Gospels of Matthew, Mark, Luke and John to get factual information about Jesus.

In a survey on religious belief made on the campus of the University of New South Wales in 1980, fewer than 30% of the thousand students interviewed said they had read a Gospel. More than 70% had never really investigated the person of Jesus. If you are in those categories you owe it to yourself to look for yourself. There is no substitute for the Gospels.

In fact, so startling are the sayings of Jesus that if there is no truth to them, it really puts Him into the 'odd' category.

c)   The giver of eternal life

On more than one occasion He claimed to be able to give people eternal life. To a woman who was drawing water at a well He said, "Everyone who drinks of this water will be thirsty again, but whoever drinks the water I give him will never thirst. Indeed, the water I give him will become in him a spring of water welling up to eternal life" (John 4:13,14).

When a rich young ruler ran up to Jesus with the question, "Teacher, what good thing must I do to get eternal life?" Jesus ultimately answered thus: "Sell your possessions and give to the poor, and you will have treasures in heaven. Then come, follow me" (Matthew 19:16,21). Jesus *gives* eternal life. It is through *following* Him that people gain eternal life.

d)   The forgiver of sins

Another astounding claim of Jesus is that He is able to forgive sins. Mark records the incident where Jesus was teaching in a building where the crowd was so great that it was impossible to accommodate any more in the house. Four men with a paralysed friend whom they were bringing to Jesus for healing were unable to get in. Their ingenuity took them up the back stairs onto the roof where they removed enough tiles to lower their friend through the opening. As Jesus saw the man, He said to him, "Son, your sins are forgiven" (Mark 2:5). The full import of this statement was not lost on those who heard it. They recognised it as a direct claim to deity. "Why does this fellow talk like that? He's blaspheming! Who can forgive sins but God alone?" (Mark 2:7). I think they were right and wrong. Right in recognising that only God can forgive sins. But wrong in failing to recognise that Jesus was God, the Son, in their midst.

e)   The judge of all the world

I think probably the boldest of all Jesus' sayings is recorded in Matthew's Gospel in chapter 25:31-46. In this passage, Jesus claims that He and He alone will judge all mankind on the day of judgment. His claim is that He will separate people into two groups as a shepherd separates sheep from goats. The basis of the division is on their attitude to Him and the nature of the division will have permanent repercussions. He will say to some, "Come, you who are blessed by my Father; take your inheritance, the kingdom prepared for you since the creation of the world" (Matthew 25:34). But to others He will say, "Depart from me, you who are cursed, into the eternal fire prepared for the devil and his angels" (Matthew 25:41).

It is such a stark saying. Yet His claims are even greater.

f)   Lord and God

John, in his Gospel, tells of a discussion which Jesus had with the Jewish leaders. Jesus called on them to recognise that He had come from God. They claimed that as children of Abraham they were God's children and were in no danger. Jesus replied that if they were true children of Abraham they would recognise Him, for as He said, "Your father Abraham rejoiced at the thought of seeing my day; he saw it and was glad."

"You are not yet fifty years old," the Jews said to Him, "and you have seen Abraham?"

"I tell you the truth," Jesus answered, "before Abraham was born, I am!" (John 8:56-58). It was a claim to be God. The Jews understood it well. Thousands of years before, when the Jews were in captivity in Egypt, Moses was chosen by God to lead them out to freedom. Moses was apprehensive about his ability to do this and said to God:

"Suppose I go to the Israelites [Jews] and say to them. 'The God of your fathers has sent me to you,' and they ask me, 'what is his name?' Then what shall I tell them?

God said to Moses, "I am who I am. This is what you are to say to the Israelites: I AM has sent me to you" (Exodus 3:13,14).

When Jesus said, "Before Abraham was, I am", He was claiming to be God who spoke with Moses thousands of years before. The Jewish people recognised the claim and believing it to be blasphemous set out to execute Jesus.

After Jesus had risen from the dead Thomas fell at His feet and said, "My Lord and my God" (John 20:28). Instead of rebuking him Jesus commended him and all who subsequently acknowledge Him as Lord and God. Again it is a direct claim to deity.

Did anyone ever make such ego-centred claims? The bread of life — the ultimate satisfier; the light of the world — the life director; the eternal life giver; the forgiver of sins; the judge of all the world; Lord and God. Indeed so absolute are the sayings of Jesus that He really leaves us very little room for manoeuvring. In the light of His claims you cannot say, "What an interesting person — do have another cup of coffee." It is clear that if Jesus is not right in the understanding of who He is then He is very badly mistaken. Indeed so badly mistaken as to be mentally deranged or worse a 'con' man on a grand scale. For my part I am convinced that His claim is able to be sustained and I invite you to read the Gospels and look for yourself.

The strange thing about the ego-centricity of Jesus' claims is that stark as they are, they are all directed at our welfare. Former boxer Mohammed Ali constantly says "I am the greatest." Yet he isn't claiming to be able to do anything for me. He leaves me where I am or maybe makes me feel inferior. But Jesus is very different. It is as if He is saying "I am the greatest and look what I can do for you."

He says that because He is the bread of life then we can be satisfied. Since He is the light of the world, we needn't be in the dark. Since He is the giver of eternal life we can share eternity with Him. Since He is the forgiver of sins we can have the guilty consciences dealt with. Since He is the judge of all the world we need not fear the judgment day. It is as if a skilful surgeon is saying, "Don't worry it's a simple operation; you need have no fear. I've done it hundreds of times." It is an ego-centric statement, yet because it is factual it fills us with confidence.

What is there about Jesus which makes His otherwise outrageous claims believable? If I had made them you wouldn't bother with me for a minute.

2. HIS BELIEVABLE ACTIONS

Although the sayings of Jesus are so ego-centric, when we see Him in action we are taken completely by surprise. He is so kind, so thoughtful, so generous and what is more He is so people-oriented. He seems quite unconcerned about Himself. His main pre-occupation is in helping people.

A man with leprosy came to Jesus and said to Him, "If you are willing, you can make me clean." Jesus reached out His hand, touched the kneeling man and said, "I am willing. Be clean!" In this demonstration of loving reassurance, the man was healed (Mark 1:40,41).

On one occasion He had been so busy in a programme of healing and teaching that those close to Him virtually said, "If you carry on like this you'll have a breakdown" (Mark 3:21). I think His attitude to people is best summed up in this statement: "When he saw the crowds, he had compassion on them, because they were harassed and helpless, like sheep without a shepherd" (Matthew 9:36). In fact so impressive is Jesus that He has inspired many people to perform acts of self-sacrificing service to mankind.

The Jesus of the Gospels seems so unconcerned about Himself and so absorbed in others that we tend to forget how self-centred the sayings of Jesus really are. What a strange contradiction He appears to be. I have known many self-centred people in my time, yet I have never met one of them who wanted to spend his life in unselfish service for others. In fact, it has been the exact opposite. They want others to spend themselves in service to them! I have also been fortunate in my life to have met people whose lives have been given in self-sacrificing devotion to others. They have been marked by their deep humility, and seem to be unconscious of their greatness. In Jesus both are combined. Yet, they seem to be perfectly balanced and quite believable. Some of His claims are in line with this life of humble service. "I am the good shepherd," He said, "the good shepherd lays down His life for the sheep" (John 10:11). Indeed it is through His ultimate sacrifice that Jesus promises to rescue us from our sins.

What a strange man He is. It is as if we have in one person the sayings of a complete self-centred person welded together with the self-sacrificing life of a Mother Theresa of Calcutta, yet the person is not a Jekyll and Hyde character, He is well balanced. Could it just be because He was who He claimed to be? Being God the Son, He is right about life and life after death. Being God, the Son, He never tires of loving the world He made and the people in it, nor does He tire of serving them as their creator and sustainer.

The well balanced man
One of the most challenging aspects of the life of Jesus of Nazareth is that He is so well balanced in the life situation. I find it very difficult to be balanced. I often

seem to be sentimental and soft when strength is called for, or else hard like granite when understanding and compassion are needed. At other times I honestly don't know what to do. Let me give an example of what I mean.

Several years ago while driving along a straight stretch of road, I stopped to give a hitch-hiker a lift. While the car was stationary another car ran into the back of me. I was genuinely surprised, to say the least. I got out to survey the damage done. My neat little sedan had the boot all crumpled up like tissue paper. His old 'bomb' had a slight dent which sprang back into place when we pulled it! By a mighty effort I managed to control myself and say, "Whatever happened?"

"I didn't see you," he replied.

"Have you had trouble with your eyes before tonight? (not kind!). Anyway let's not waste time now, get out your licence and we can take down the necessary information."

"I don't have a licence," he said. My blood pressure rose by another ten points.

"What do you mean, you don't have a licence?"

"I'm not old enough," he said sheepishly, "I'm only fifteen."

"You couldn't get one if you were fifty-five! I suppose you've stolen that car, have you?"

"No," he replied.

"Give it a break, pal. Do you ask me to believe that someone lent you a car knowing full well that you don't have a licence? You must think I'm mad. You're in big trouble. Your father will be in trouble and so is the person who lent you the car."

At that moment he burst into tears.

"The guy next door lent it to me to take my girl for a spin just along River Road and back again. My dad doesn't know. Please don't dob me in. I was really showing off. I promise I won't do it again."

I'm a soft touch when people cry. But I'd like you to tell me what is the right course of action to take. I can think of several ways to act, and what's more they all in one way seem right.

I could let him go and make good the damage myself. I could get the police and let the law take its course. I could go home and see his father and the chap next door and let them make good the damage etc. Or I could do a combination of the last two. In real life it's easier to recognise balanced people than it is to be one.

As you read the Gospels, notice how truly balanced Jesus is. I think the best illustration of this is recorded for us in John's Gospel. A group of Pharisees and teachers of the Law brought a woman, accused of adultery, to Jesus to ask what should be done to her. Adultery, at that time, was a capital offence amongst the Jews. However, since the Romans had occupied Palestine, they had taken from the Jews the right to execute anyone. They came with a question to trick Jesus. When asked what should happen to her He appeared to have two options either of which was a 'no-win' situation. If He said "free her" He would be in trouble with the Jewish religious authorities. If He said "execute her" He would be in trouble with the Romans. However, that was only the surface problem. What was He to do with these men who didn't give a hoot about the woman or even what was right? How are hypocrites to be dealt with? They said to Jesus, "Teacher, this woman was caught in the act of adultery. In the Law, Moses commanded us to stone such women. Now what do you say?" (John 8:4,5).

I have lived a fairly sheltered life but even I know that it's not all that easy to find someone in the very act of adultery. What were they doing? Peeping through key holes or had they deliberately set her up? The latter, I think. How should they be dealt with. They were about to lynch her by stoning.

Now think for a moment about the woman. What should happen to her? The whole incident bristles with problems. What is the well balanced person to do. I know what I would have done. I'm sure I would have blasted the Pharisees. I would have let the woman go. What would you have done?

If you know the story, you know what Jesus did. But if you don't, ponder on how really clever and beautifully balanced Jesus is. "If anyone of you is without sin, let him be the first to throw a stone at her" (John 8:7). Isn't that a clever statement? So simple yet so revealing. It is so easy to know what to do when it is someone else's problem, but it is so hard to think it out quickly oneself, isn't it?

Jesus' reply was so stunning that, ". . those who heard began to go away one at a time, the older ones first" (John 8:9). Finally Jesus was left alone with the woman.

"Where are they? Has no one condemned you?" He asked.

"No one, sir."

"Then neither do I condemn you," Jesus declared. "Go now and leave your life of sin" (John 8:10,11).

See what He does. In these few sentences He unmasks hypocrisy so that men see themselves for what they are. He upholds the rightness of the law and acts with love and compassion. And all in two short sentences. Give it a try yourself sometime — it's easier said than done.

Such is the person of Jesus in the four Gospels that again and again I find myself saying, "That's right. If only we would behave like that, this world would be a marvellous place in which to live."

Jesus is no eccentric, yet He is able to see through the folly of believing life is about material possessions. In our best moments we know that is true, yet in our worst we persist in believing that if we could get more things we would be happy. Jesus has a wonderful story about it all. I'll try and paraphrase it into a modern setting. It goes like this:

"A certain businessman had made a small fortune by hard work and careful investment. He and his wife had decided to retire early. They had bought a block of home units on the Gold Coast and were going to occupy one overlooking the ocean, lease the rest and live comfortably on the income. They were giving a party to say 'good-bye' to their friends. He was on the veranda of his city suburban home with a long cool glass of refreshment. "What a lucky man you are," he thought, "you have everything you need. You can eat, drink and be merry." A terrible pain racked across his chest and he died before they could get him to intensive care. Who will get the home units now?

"So it is with everyone who puts their trust in riches and isn't rich towards God." You may like to read the original in Luke 12:16-21.

Let me encourage you to read the Sermon on the Mount (Matthew Chapters 5 to 7) and see for yourself if you are not impressed by the balance of this man.

A really good man

One night I was twiddling the dial of my transistor radio and picked up a station where authors were being interviewed about their books and their styles. I don't know who the author was, but the interviewer said to him, "Do you make your heroes good and your villains bad?"

The author laughed and said, "I try to make all my characters *real.*" I thought to myself, "How right you are." Real people are never really good or really bad but have both good and bad qualities which are held in tension. Have you ever noticed in literature that you never find a really good person who is believable. Sometimes you meet "Pollyanna" type people but they are always too good to be true and the better they are the less believable they become.

Sometimes in fiction we have unbalanced people going around doing good, as in Don Quixote. They will some-times seem believable. But Jesus is not such a 'goody' as to be unbelievable. Nor is He unbalanced. The Jesus we find in the pages of the Gospels is a thoroughly good person while also being thoroughly believable. So I want to ask: Were the authors who wrote the Gospels just clever at characterisation? Or could it just be that the person they saw, heard and lived with, really was the perfect man — the man just like God — and rather than being dull and boring He turned out to be fine and exciting, appealing yet very challenging?

What a strange mixture He is. He *humbly* claims to be God! He is ego-centricly concerned about others! He cleverly refutes His enemies. He is good without being 'saccharine sweet'! He claims to conquer the world by His own execution!

Who is He? His followers were convinced He was God the Son and worshipped Him as Lord. Do the facts allow you to believe either of the other two alternatives? Is He mad? Is He a deceiver?

3. HIS RESURRECTION FROM DEATH

So unusual is it for a person to return to life after death, that we must examine the evidence closely in three separate categories.
a)   What the papers say
b)   What the disciples did
c)   No eye-witness update

a)   What the papers say

All four Gospel writers tell of the eye-witness accounts of those who saw Jesus alive and well after His crucifixion and burial.

Matthew:
   *Jesus appeared to Mary Magdalene and Mary the mother of Jesus (Matthew 28:1-10).
   *Jesus appeared to the eleven remaining disciples some of whom found it hard to believe, but all of whom worshipped Him (Matthew 28:16-20).

Mark:

  *The tomb was empty and a young man in white robes announced to the women who had come to anoint Jesus' body:

  "You are looking for Jesus the Nazarene, who was crucified. He has risen! He is not here. See the place where they laid him. But go, tell his disciples and Peter, 'He is going ahead of you into Galilee. There you will see him, just as he told you'" (Mark 16:6,7).

Luke:

  *Recorded the same incident as Mark (Luke 24:1-8).
  *Peter went to the tomb and found it open with the grave clothes still there but no body (Luke 24:12).
  *Jesus appeared to two unnamed disciples on the way to Emmaus. He walked and talked with them on this seven mile journey (Luke 24:13-32).
  *Jesus appeared to Simon (Peter's other name) (Luke 24:34).
  * So that they may be completely convinced that He wasn't some ghost or vision, Jesus invited the disciples to touch Him (Luke 24:37-43).

John:

  *Mary of Magdala first saw the empty tomb, then saw Jesus (John 20:1,2,10-18).
  *The disciples, except Thomas, saw Jesus (John 20:19-23).
  *Thomas was sceptical and declared that he would only believe if he could see and touch the nail marks in Jesus' hands and the spear wound in His side (John 20:25).
  *Jesus appeared again to the disciples while Thomas was present, and allowed Thomas to prove in his own way, the reality of the resurrection. Thomas was convinced (John 20:24-28).

*Jesus appeared to the disciples at the Sea of Tiberias (John 21·1-4)

In a letter to the Church at Corinth about twenty years after the death of Jesus, Paul produced a list of people who saw Jesus after His death and resurrection.

Paul:

*". . . he [Jesus] appeared to Peter, and then to the Twelve. After that, he appeared to more than five hundred of the brothers at the same time, most of whom are still living, though some have fallen asleep. Then he appeared to James, then to all the apostles, and last of all he appeared to me. . ." (1 Corinthians 15:5-8).

If these accounts are not factual then they are a wicked deception, for they contain most impressive lists of eye-witnesses. If not true, what could be the motive behind it? There was everything to be lost, and nothing to be gained by falsifying the facts.

What the disciples did

As well as the eye-witness records two aspects of the lives of the disciples after the resurrection are noteworthy.

First the disciples were changed from weak, cowardly men into brave, courageous witnesses to Jesus and His resurrection. At the time of Jesus' arrest they all forsook Him and fled (Mark 14:50). Yet within a matter of months they were prepared to stand before the Council which had condemned Jesus to death and all boldly resisted the advice given them not to preach about Him. What had changed them? The unshakable certainty that Jesus had risen from the dead that He was alive and was both Lord and Christ (Acts 4:10).

No eye-witness update

On the early morning newscast a leading member of the government was reported to have made an outrageous statement. The government at the time was not in such good shape and it occurred to me that if their spokesman had really made the reported claims, then the government deserved to fall.

Keenly interested, I continued to listen at hourly intervals. The statement was repeated several times. I listened to the news on another station — there was no mention of it! The first reporter must have been mistaken I decided. By mid-morning, the original statement had been drastically revised, and by noon it had been so altered as to be no longer newsworthy.

The early preaching about Jesus' resurrection met with scepticism and unbelief (Acts 17:32-34). The unbelief was centered on the fact of the resurrection of Jesus. The apostles found it as difficult to persuade people in the first century, as we do in the twentieth. However, there is no evidence that they updated the message by dropping it, modifying it or soft-peddling it. If they had invented the whole story to try to influence more people, then it was the wrong move. As pro-Christian propaganda it was and is a dismal failure, because it has become the most difficult to believe of all facts and aspects of Christianity.

No, the apostles would not budge. Why? Because they were convinced that they had seen Jesus alive after His death. God had in fact made Him both Lord and Christ (Acts 2:36).

At the beginning of this chapter, I made the point that any investigation of Christianity was basically an investigation of the person of Jesus. I have tried to show what a really unique person He is. Even so, I have not given full weight to the way in which the Gospel writers describe Jesus. They were convinced that He was, and is, none other than God the Son. Ultimately, there is no substitute for reading the Gospels. Is it possible in the light of the evidence to believe that He was deluded, a lunatic? Is it possible to believe that He was a fraud, a liar? Is there any other possibility but that He is who He claimed to be, the Son of God?

In addition to the aspects of Jesus' life which we have examined, the Gospel writers also see Jesus as Lord in His creation. He fulfils the expectations which they had from reading the Old Testament. That is the subject of the next chapter. . .

CHAPTER EIGHT

The Lord in His World

All four Gospel writers were convinced that Jesus Christ was really God's unique Son. Mark opened his Gospel with the words: "The beginning of the Gospel about Jesus Christ, the Son of God" (Mark 1:1). He ended his Gospel with the Roman centurion surpervising Jesus' crucifixion and saying, "Surely this man was the Son of God" (Mark 15:39).

The other three were equally convinced. They saw in Jesus the one who in every way fitted the Old Testament description of God. In describing Jesus as He was, they show a picture of the Lord in His creation. He is in control of every situation.

Better than a weather forecaster

On one occasion after Jesus had been teaching from Peter's boat they set out to cross the sea of Galilee. It was evening and Jesus had fallen asleep in the back of the boat. A severe wind storm arose so that the disciples despaired of life itself, in spite of the fact that they were experienced fishermen who knew the lake and knew their boats. It was more than a breeze on Sydney Harbour. One of them shook Jesus with the rebuke, "Don't you care if we all perish?" Jesus stood up in the boat and commanded the winds and the waves: "Quiet! Be still!"

Here is Mark's description of what followed. "The wind died down and it was completely calm. He said to his disciples, 'Why are you so afraid? Do you still have no faith?' They were terrified and asked each other —

"Who is this? Even the wind and the waves obey him!'"
(Mark 4:35-41).

Jesus is shown to us as master in His world. Certainly
no ordinary man can do what Jesus had just done. Any
day you are tempted to think you are the master of the
creation take a ferry trip from Circular Quay across to
Manly, or across the Channel from Dover, and as you
come to where the swell is greatest have a go! Command
the waves to be still. (I would advise you to do it quietly
out at the stern of the ship where no one can hear you.)

I don't want to give the impression that Jesus was some
super trickster. No doubt when the disciples saw what
He did, they recalled the words of the Old Testament
book of Psalms written hundreds of years before, where
God is described like this:

"O Lord God Almighty, who is like you?
    You are mighty, O Lord, and your
        faithfulness surrounds you.
    You rule over the surging sea;
        when its waves mount up, you still
            them." (Psalm 89:8,9).

Or again when describing people caught in a storm at
sea:

"Then they cried out to the Lord in
    their trouble,
    and he brought them out of their
        distress.
He stilled the storm to a whisper;
    the waves of the sea were hushed.
They were glad when it grew calm,
    and he guided them to their desired
        haven." (Psalm 107:28-30).

When we come to Jesus we are with no ordinary person.
He is shown as the Lord in control over the creation.

God visiting His people
The Gospels abound with descriptions of Jesus healing
people's bodies and minds. Those who were blind re-

ceived their sight. The crippled were cured, leprous people were healed.

It is important to note that Jesus was doing this because it was exactly the way God promised to act on behalf of His people. In the Old Testament book Isaiah, God is described as one who will reassure His people:

Strengthen the feeble hands,
    steady the knees that give way;
say to those with fearful hearts;
    "Be strong, do not fear,
your God will come,
    he will come with vengeance;
with divine retribution
    he will come to save you."

Then will the eyes of the blind be
    opened
    and the ears of the deaf unstopped.
Then will the lame leap like a deer,
    and the tongue of the dumb shout
        for joy. (Isaiah 35:3-6).

When John the Baptist was arrested he sent a message to Jesus to ask Jesus to reassure him that He, Jesus, really was God's Messiah who would rescue His people. Jesus gave a demonstration of the passage quoted, and used it to identify Himself. This is how Luke described it:

". . . the men came to Jesus and said, 'John the Baptist has sent us to you to ask, "Are you the one who was to come, or should we expect someone else?" ' At that time Jesus cured many who had diseases, sicknesses and evil spirits, and gave sight to many who were blind. So he replied to the messengers, 'Go back and report to John what you have seen and heard: The blind receive sight, and lame walk, those who have leprosy are cured, the deaf hear, the dead are raised and the good news is preached to the poor' " (Luke 7:20-22).

Better than a specialist

There is no doubt that Jesus expected people to recognise that He was God's Messiah by these healings. Some did. Luke recognised an incident where a Roman centurion requested Jesus to heal his servant. He sent this request through the Jewish elders to urge Jesus to do so. "The Roman," they assured Him, "is noble. He loves our nation and has built us a synagogue." Jesus agreed to go with them but as they travelled on the way the centurion sent a message to Jesus.

"Lord don't trouble yourself, for I do not deserve to have you come under my roof. That is why I did not even consider myself worthy to come to you. But say the word, and my servant will be healed. For I myself am a man under authority, with soldiers under me. I tell this one, 'Go', and he goes; and that one, 'Come', and he comes. I say to my servant, 'Do this,' and he does it."

"When Jesus heard this, he was amazed at him, and turning to the crowd following him, he said, 'I tell you, I have not found such great faith even in Israel.' Then the man who had been sent returned to the house and found the servant well" (Luke 7:6-10).

The Roman centurion recognised in Jesus the kind of authority that placed Him in a unique category. All Jesus needed to do was speak the word of command and the centurion would be healed. Subsequent events showed that this faith was not misplaced.

Better than a clairvoyant

I have already referred to the incident where the paralysed man was lowered through the roof that Jesus might heal him. When Jesus said to the paralysed man, "Son, your sins are forgiven," some teachers of the law who were there were *thinking to themselves*, 'He's blaspheming! Who can forgive sins but God alone?"

Mark makes a very significant comment: "Immediately Jesus *knew* in his spirit that this was *what they were thinking in their hearts"* (Mark 2:8). I cannot imagine anything so disconcerting as to be in the company of someone who knew exactly what I was thinking!

An exorcist who could

Several records of Jesus dealing with the spirit world show Him to be the master over the evil powers. In fact wherever Jesus comes into contact with destructive evil powers He immediately releases people from their oppression and slavery to such powers (see Mark 1:21-27; Matthew 8:16).

The Gospel writers give us interesting descriptions of many exorcisms. What is even more interesting is that the evil spirits recognised Jesus as God's Son. Mark tells of such an incident:

". . . a man in their synagogue who was possessed by an evil spirit cried out, 'What do you want with us, Jesus of Nazareth? Have you come to destroy us? I know who you are — the Holy One of God!'

Be quiet! said Jesus sternly. 'Come out of him!' The evil spirit shook the man violently and came out of him with a shriek.

The people were all amazed that they asked each other, 'What is this? A new teaching — and with authority! He even gives orders to evil spirits and they obey him'" (Mark 1:23-27).

Death, no problem

In the Gospels there are three separate incidents where Jesus brought people back to life. Matthew and Luke both tell of a ruler who came to Jesus with a request to heal his small child. By the time they returned, the ruler's daughter had died, but Jesus took her hand in His and commanded, "My child, get up!" The little girl sat up, well again (Matthew 9:18-25; Luke 8:49-56).

One step removed, a widow's son in the town of Nain was dead and in his coffin on the way to burial. Jesus stopped the procession. His heart went out to the grieving woman, "Don't cry," He said. Then He went up and touched the coffin, and those carrying it stood still. He said, "Young man, I say to you, get up!" The dead man sat up and began to talk and Jesus gave him back to his mother (Luke 7:11-17).

I have been to hundreds of funerals since I was ordained to the ministry, and yet I can truly say it has never once occurred to me to rap on the casket and say — "Young man, I say to you, get up!" — and the reason is obvious; I am not Lord of life and death.

These two incidents are remarkable enough, yet the one recorded by John in his Gospel is even more so. Lazarus, a friend of Jesus, was ill. It was serious and his sisters, Mary and Martha, sent for Jesus to heal their brother. Jesus delayed and Lazarus had died. When He arrived at their home in Bethany, Martha reproached Him saying "If only you had been here my brother would not have died." Her sister, Mary, later said the same thing. In response, Jesus made two extremely dramatic statements. First He announced that their brother would rise from the dead. I say startling because he had been dead and buried for four days. The second startling statement is this: "I am the resurrection and the life. He who believes in me will live, even though he dies; and whoever lives and believes in me will never die" (John 11:25).

They went to the graveyard. The man was buried in a cave with a stone rolled across the mouth as was the custom. Jesus commanded that the stone be removed. Martha was in despair, "Don't do it, his body will have started to decompose — the stench of death will be on him."

Jesus said to her, "Didn't I tell you if you believed in me you would see the glory of God." They rolled away the stone and after Jesus prayed he called with a loud voice, "Lazarus, come out!"

John described the event — "The dead man came out, his hands and feet wrapped with strips of linen, and a

cloth around his face" (John 11:44). (I'll bet the hairs
stood up on the backs of their necks that day!)

To be in the presence of Jesus of Nazareth was to be
in the presence of no ordinary man. We are in the presence of the Lord of life and Master of death. In the last
book of the Bible the apostle John described a vision he
had of the risen Jesus. We are not surprised to hear Jesus
describe Himself as "I am the First and the Last. I am
the Living One; I was dead, and behold I am alive for
ever and ever! And I hold the keys of death and Hades"
(Revelation 1:18).

Master and Lord over His enemies

Even at the moment of His arrest and during His trial,
although He was a prisoner and powerless, Jesus still
appeared to be in a position of strength rather than of
weakness. His trials were conducted before the High
Priest, Herod the King, and Pontius Pilate the Governor.
As I read the Gospels it appears as if it were His judges
who were on trial and not Jesus Himself. At their moment of human destiny they failed to do what was right,
and though innocent, He was condemned to die.

Just when they thought they had dealt with Him forever, they discovered that they could not effect a permanent death. He came back from the dead. I often
wonder how Jesus' accusers, judges and executioners must
have felt when they received the news of His resurrection
and that all attempts to find the body had failed. I wonder
if they looked over their shoulders late at night when
climbing the stairs on their way to bed.

The picture which the Gospel writers show us is of a
very impressive and remarkable person indeed. They are
convinced that He is God's unique Son.

Thomas states it for them in his admission "My Lord
and my God!" (John 20:28). I too have been convinced
that this is the right way to understand this person in
history.

Face to face

John tells us in his Gospel that he became convinced that Jesus was truly God's Son and that is exactly why he wrote his Gospel.

> "Jesus did many other miraculous signs in the presence of his disciples, which are not recorded in this book. But these are written that you may believe that Jesus is the Christ, the Son of God, and that by believing you may have life in his name" (John 20:30,31).

All the New Testament writers agree with John in their assessment of Jesus. Several of these writers were personal friends of Jesus. They had been disciples of His from the beginning. They lived with Him, moved around the country side with Him, ate with Him, and they worked from a common purse (designed to disrupt any good friendship!). That they were loyal is to be expected. But that they described Him, who had been under such close scrutiny, as the Son of God is remarkable. The thing about our friends is that they know our weaknesses only too well and yet love us in spite of those faults. The disciples knew Jesus thoroughly and the more they got to know Him the more they became convinced that He was perfect.

However, no amount of my writing is a substitute for your reading of the originals. The Gospels are readily available in modern translations. You should look for yourself.

Two problems

Before you begin this investigation, there are two questions which should be faced. One is more easily dealt with than the other.

The first is: *Can I really trust the Gospels?* Are they sufficiently accurate for me to be able to get a clear and consistent picture of Jesus?

The second is: *Can I really trust myself to be honest in an investigation?*

Let's look at the second question which is probably the more difficult one.

Can I trust myself?

Only you can deal with this question. It is personal and private.

When I was first confronted with the gospel and its full implications my difficulty was not whether or not it was right, I secretly believed it was. My problem was that I just didn't *want* it to be right. I didn't want Jesus to be Lord over my life. I wanted to be free and independent. As I've already described it, I wanted to be my own God and the best way to do that is to do away with God. So I pretended God didn't exist. That had a very marked effect on my investigation. I didn't let the evidence mould my opinion. My mind was already made up. There was no way in which I was approaching it objectively. I didn't allow the facts to persuade me. I wanted the result to be negative because I didn't want to change my way of life. Sir Kenneth Clark, for many years director of the National Gallery London, clearly illustrates this in the second volume of his autobiography:

"I lived in solitude, surrounded by books on the history of religion, which have always been my favourite reading. This may help to account for a curious episode that took place on one of my stays in the Villino. I had a religious experience. It took place in the Church of San Lorenzo, but did not seem to be connected with the harmonious beauty of the architecture. I can only say that for a few minutes my whole being was irradiated by a kind of heavenly joy, far more intense than anything I had known before. This state of mind lasted for several months, and, wonderful though it was, it posed an awkward problem in terms of action. My life was far from blameless: I would have to reform. My family would think I was going mad, and perhaps after all, it *was* a delusion, for I was in every way unworthy of receiving such a flood of grace. Gradually the effect wore off, and I made no effort to retain it. I think I was right; I was too deeply embedded in the world to change course. But that I had 'felt the finger of God' I am quite sure, and, although the memory of this experience has faded, it still helps me to understand the joys of the saints."[1]

Sir Kenneth Clark tells us with disarming honesty that it was not for want of evidence that he did not move into a true relationship with God, indeed he received an experience which I have never had, there were other personal factors which got in the way.

I was urging a young man at a university mission to take a Gospel and read it. He told me he hadn't ever read one, and didn't want to take one even then. "What have you got to lose?" I asked.

"Everything," he replied, "it might turn out to be true."

I really understood what he meant. I'd been there before. The question, 'Can I trust myself to look honestly?' is hard. Much harder than it appears. If Jesus is Lord and alive today, then I have no real reason for not becoming a true Christian. I need to be open to change. I need to approach my investigation humbly lest in passing judgment on Jesus I find the tables turned on me. Some people have found that they are able to pray a prayer like this — *O God, if you really are there, please help me to investigate the person of Jesus honestly, humbly and in such a way that I will be prepared to change if necessary.* It may help you, but I should point out that even to do that, rather implies that God is there already. Don't let me trick you, and try not to trick yourself.

1. *The Other Side,* Kenneth Clark, John Murray.

CHAPTER NINE

Can I Trust the Gospels?

When it comes to a genuine search for God, we need to take care to look in the right place. Some people have told me that they draw near to God on the beach or while walking in the bushland. I cannot pass judgment on the experiences of others, but we must take care that we don't confuse God with a feeling of well being. It may be that it wasn't God we encountered at the beach but the feeling of relief which comes to everyone when we 'get away from it all'.

Imagine one day finding a man with his head in the oven. "What are you doing?" you ask.

"Making a phone call," he replies. You may well wonder if you have stumbled into a Laurel and Hardy movie. I know it's absurd. But so often when I ask people about their search for God they seem to me to be looking in the wrong place. It is because of this that I have been encouraging a careful investigation of the person of Jesus. He claims to show us and tell us exactly what God is like, but where do we get accurate information about Jesus?

Only in the Bible?

We know enough from non-Christian historians to be able to establish the fact that Jesus of Nazareth lived in Palestine in the first century. Pliny[1] the Younger was appointed by the Emperor Trajan to govern Bithynia (modern Turkey) in the year AD112. Among his many letters to the emperor is an interesting one describing

1. Pliny, *Epistles* 10.96

the Christians and their gatherings. It is clear that by this date Christianity had spread widely in the province. Tacitus, a Roman and a contemporary of Pliny, tells in his *Annals* that the term 'Christian' comes from Christ who was executed in the reign of Tiberius by the Prefect Pontius Pilate.[1] It is clear from his works that he has no sympathy with the Christians at all but he knows where it had its origin.

Josephus, a Jewish historian, gives us further information in two of his works — *Antiquities of the Jews* (AD93) and *Jewish Wars* (AD75). In these works we meet many of the persons mentioned in the New Testament — Pilate, Annas, Caiaphas, Herod and others. Josephus tells us about John the Baptist as well as Jesus. He tells us that Jesus was a "doer of marvellous deeds, a teacher of men who received the truth with pleasure. He won over many Jews and also many Greeks".[2]

He goes on to speak of Jesus' death and resurrection and of the group called Christians who came into being because of him.[3]

In his book, "Jesus and Christian Origins Outside the New Testament" (Hodder 1974), F.F. Bruce gave an impressive collection of quotations about Christians from other ancient historians although they were not Christians themselves.

We can establish a certain amount of information about Jesus from these men but our detailed information about the person of Jesus comes from the four Gospels, Matthew, Mark, Luke and John in the Bible.

A word about what the Bible is may not go astray. I find that people often react emotionally to the Bible — sometimes negatively, sometimes positively, but generally without quite knowing why. Some people react by

1. Tacitus, *Annals* 15.44
2. Josephus, *Antiquities* 18.33
3. See *Runaway World* Michael Green, IVP.

saying, "If it's in the Bible it must be true", while others hold exactly the opposite view.

The Bible is a collection of sixty-six small books which have been bound together in one volume for the convenience of Christians. In the Old Testament there are thirty-nine books which were written before Jesus Christ was born. They were written by a variety of authors from various cultural backgrounds, spanning hundreds of years. The New Testament contains the remaining twenty-seven books which were written in the first century AD. They are about Jesus and how He is to be understood and how Christians should relate to Him. The books are neither reliable nor unreliable just because they are 'in the Bible'. Christians believe they are reliable and helpful for them which is why they have been bound into a convenient and easily accessible single volume. Christians believe that the books are the inspired word of God but I am not asking *you* to believe that at this stage.

Can I really trust the Gospels?

The narratives about Jesus' life (the Gospels) claim to give us accurate information, as well as the writers' interpretations of that information. So we need to ask now: Are they, in fact, sufficiently reliable as histories for us to look at the Jesus who lived in Palestine in the first century?

Do you believe everything you read?

We are a strange mixture of gullibility and scepticism. If I say to you, "Do you believe everything you read in the newspaper? You would probably say, "No." And I would agree. However, the fact is that we usually do believe it for no other reason than that it is printed in the paper! We may be more discriminating when it comes to television advertising. We know when the salesman says "I wouldn't do this commercial if it were not true," that there's a better than even chance he is lying. However, when the newsreader appears on the box, meticulously groomed, dispensing information probably of unknown origin, but in such a cultured authoritative voice, then we will probably think what *he* says is true.

What makes an historical record accurate anyway? I would want to ask these questions. Was the writer an eyewitness to the event? If not, from where did he get his information? Do we have any verifying histories available from other authors? Were they published in the lifetime of eye-witnesses? How soon after the event were they written? Have they been transmitted accurately? Does the historian have an "axe to grind", some biased motive? Do his other utterances ring true?

When I submit the Gospels, Matthew, Mark, Luke and John to these tests, I am satisfied that they do give us a reliable history of Jesus.

Were the Gospel writers eye-witnesses?

The apostles were with Jesus during his entire ministry. Matthew and John's Gospels are eye-witness accounts. There is an old but unproven tradition that Mark's Gospel is really the apostle Peter's account, recorded for him by Mark; Luke tells us that he himself is not an eye-witness but he also tells from where he got his information.

It is clear to any reader of the four Gospels that Matthew, Mark and Luke bear a strong similarity although each has his distinctive style and aim. It remains still a matter of debate amongst New Testament scholars as to whether they copied from each other or whether they had access to some earlier documents which are now lost.

John on the other hand, is quite an independent Gospel. Apart from the death and resurrection of Jesus, he hardly duplicates any of the stories in the other Gospels. It seems as if he did not have access to the other Gospels at the time he wrote his. This means that we have at least two completely independent histories which makes very valuable evidence. Often a document from antiquity stands alone with no other against which to check it. A good exercise would be to read Luke's Gospel and then John's. Then ask yourself, "Is the Jesus as portrayed in one, the same as in the other?" I am convinced He is, and it has given me much confidence in the Gospels as accurate, first hand eye-witness accounts.

As you read through Matthew and John you will see the eye-witness touches about them. Matthew 28:17 is a good example. "When they saw him, they worshipped him; but some doubted." The piece of information, "but some doubted" is an interesting sidelight. It doesn't do anything for the story or for the 'cause'. If anything it weakens the case for the resurrection. So why does Matthew insert it'? Because he remembered it like that! Notice the eye-witness touch in John 6:10. It is the description of the feeding of the five thousand. "There was plenty of grass in that place, and the men sat down, about five thousand of them." No doubt you would remember the lush green of a pleasant spring picnic and even comment on it, but would you bother to say so if you hadn't been there?

Several years ago a well known author and television script writer, Tony Morphett, became a Christian. Before that, by his own choice, he had been an atheist. A set of circumstances occurred which resulted in his reading the New Testament. He said that he was impressed with the Gospels: "I had spent all my working life writing scripts which were either documentary or fiction. When I came to the Gospels, I recognised that they were not fiction. They were documentary."[1]

Paul Barnett, Lecturer in New Testament history at Macquarie University and the University of Sydney states, "While the Gospels have many distinctive features, they are in broad terms recognisable examples of history writ-

---

1. See *A Hole in My Ceiling*, Tony Morphett, Hodder and Stoughton (Aust)

ers of their period. It is unhelpful and untrue to regard them merely as religious or theological works. They are also unmistakably historical in character. As historical sources of this period, they are just as valuable to the general historian as Josephus. Except unlike Josephus they are focused on one person and for a brief period."

Luke, on the other hand, tells us that he is not an eye-witness. The introduction to his Gospel shows historical method: —

"Many have undertaken to draw up an account of the things that have been fulfilled among us, just as they were handed down to us by those who from the first were eye-witnesses and servants of the word. There-fore, since I myself have carefully investigated every-thing from the beginning, it seemed good also to me to write an orderly account for you, most excellent Theophilus, so that you may know the certainty of the things you have been taught" (Luke 1:1-4).

It is an interesting introduction written to his patron Theophilus of whom we know nothing. But its value lies in several areas. We know that at the time of writing this Gospel, there were many accounts of the sayings and actions of Jesus available. These accounts claimed to have been handed down from eye-witnesses. Luke is anxious that his patron should know "the certainty" about what he had heard. He wants him to be sure, so the most practical way to do that is to go back to square one him-self. He has gone back to "eye-witnesses" so that "from the beginning" he might record an "orderly account". That is the writer's stated aim. His historical method is sound and tells us the purpose of this book.

You may be interested to know that some of those other accounts have survived. The early church rejected them as accurate accounts either because they could not establish who the authors were or because they were proven to be forgeries.

But weren't they all biased?
It has often been said to me that the Gospel writers were

all convinced Christians and so they must be biased in their approach. This is partly true. They were thoroughly convinced that Jesus is the unique Son of God. However, the prior question is — "What caused them to be convinced?" John tells us that he has become convinced about Jesus and he has recorded the reasons so that we can be convinced (John 20:31).

The Gospel writers, unlike many editorial writers, present their case and their personal interest and conviction right from the start and invite us to examine their conclusions. Sometimes they record incidents from the life of Jesus, sometimes they write editorial comments. It is easy to spot the difference. They make no effort to hide it. Most people don't go to the trouble to write a book unless they are really interested in the subject, and interest in the subject leads to greater attention to detail.

One of the characteristics which the Gospel writers claim for Jesus is that He was a person who told the truth and encouraged others to do so. Jesus claimed to be the embodiment of truth. He taught His disciples to love truth and to prize it highly. To be a disciple of Jesus means to do as Jesus did. Their interest in Jesus was likely to cause them to take greater care to check the facts than to make them up.

There is no doubt that they were convinced and completely absorbed by their subject. This is not the same as saying they must have been exaggerating because they were so convinced. If that were the case, it would mean we would never be able to get accurate information except from disinterested people. It's not on! Disinterested people can often give us inaccurate accounts due to their lack of interest which causes them not to take care.

When were they published?

Suppose we were at a discussion group and at the end of the night we each wrote an account of the evening. There would be bound to be variations as some remembered incidents which others either didn't notice or forgot. If we met the next night and read our accounts together we would be able to enlarge them and correct them. Someone would say, "No, it wasn't exactly like that, was it? or "Didn't Tom say . . ." and so the process would go on.

Suppose on the other hand we sealed the accounts and deposited them for safe keeping until after we had all died. If they were then opened and read, it might be possible to get a fairly accurate account of that night if the accounts were substantially the same. However, there would be less chance of certainty if there were wide variations in the accounts; indeed we could never know. All history is like this. We need eye-witnesses to write (or tell) their accounts, but we also need their accounts to go into circulation while other eye-witnesses are still alive.

When we come to the Gospels and ask these questions we find we can be satisfied. New Testament scholars are convinced that all four Gospels were written before the close of the first century AD. Some believe they were available within thirty years of the death of Jesus, certainly within the lifetime of the eye-witnesses. It was interesting for me to notice some years ago, that three-quarters of a century after the event, there were still enough Boer War veterans alive in Australia to refute an inaccurate history of the Boer War. Memories span a long time.

When I was first ordained I worked in outback northern New South Wales. I met a very old lady who told me how as a young girl she had been brought with her family by bullock dray eight hundred kilometers from Sydney, and how her father had pioneered the property on which she was then living. She was spanning in memory a period of some sixty years. She was an old lady and the story had, I'm sure, been told many times before.

Several years later, I met a man, also elderly, who I learned had come with the same party but a different family. There was no doubt in my mind that I was hearing the *same* story through a different eye-witness. My own mother in her old age would tell the stories of her childhood again and again. They never varied. In fact, towards the end we knew them so well we could prompt her when she forgot where she was up to in the story.

Some people have objected to the fact that thirty years between the Jesus events and the writing of the Gospels really is a long time. Is it not possible that people would have forgotten what really took place? It is possible that some small details may have been forgotten. But not the important facts of the events, for at least two reasons: because they were regularly retold and because they were memorable.

1. They were regularly retold

It wasn't as if the writers sat down one day some thirty years after the events and wrote them down. They were telling the stories of Jesus from the moment He went back into heaven. A New Testament book called the Acts of the Apostles gives us a record of these. They were not conscious of being history 'writers'. They were convinced that the risen Jesus was able to bring men and women into relationship with God and they wanted people to enjoy that new life.

In spite of the constant re-telling of the Jesus incidents there are still interesting variations between all four Gospels. I would have thought that in thirty years of re-telling, all variations would have been ironed out, yet the writers did not attempt to rationalise their accounts. They bear sufficient differences in detail, while agreeing on the essential facts. They show how one eye-witness remembers what others did not notice or thought irrelevant. Such variations in the text speak of authenticity rather than the opposite. They are quite remarkable documents.

2. They were so memorable

Thirty years is forever when you are twenty! It is much shorter when you are fifty. Plenty of significant incidents can be remembered accurately for thirty years. Ask any woman married for more than thirty years to tell you about her wedding day or the birth of her first child. She will not have forgotten. She may be hazy about some details, but the important facts will be remembered.

The sayings and actions of Jesus are so very memorable. If you had witnessed Lazarus coming back to life (John 11), would it be likely that you would have forgotten it? If we had been guests at the wedding feast at Cana of Galilee and had seen the water turned to wine (John 2), there is no way we would have forgotten it.

That the writers didn't immediately put the Gospels into written form is to our advantage rather than the opposite. They really did let enough time elapse to reflect on what actually *did* take place. There was time for all the information to come to light. There is no doubt that we could write a better history of the Second World War now, than one about some contemporary world crisis. We are far enough away from one to reflect on it and for all the information to come to light. We are too close to the other to know exactly what is happening.

Have they been changed?

It's one question to ask, if the Gospels were accurate when they were first written, it is another to be sure that the ones we have today have not been changed in the last two thousand years as they have come down to us.

The Gospels were originally written in Greek. We do not have the original Gospels written by Matthew, Mark, Luke or John. Those manuscripts/parchments have been lost or were destroyed. Hand written copies were made from them to increase availability and circulation of the Gospels and to replace them as they wore out. If we did have the originals, our questions would be answered easily. All we would have to do would be to translate from them direct and compare with the modern 'handed down' translations. Any variation would immediately be evident, but it is not as easy as that.

The oldest complete Gospel we have available is believed to have been copied some time between 200-250AD. It is called the *Chester Beatty Biblical Papyri*. Earlier still is a part of John's Gospel (John 18:31-33,37) dated around130 AD, and now housed in John Rylands Library Manchester.[1]

There are at present in existence about five thousand ancient manuscripts of the New Testament. The best and most important go back to some time about 350 AD. By comparison with other works from antiquity, New Testament scholars are very fortunate. For Caesar's *Gallic War* written about 58-50 BC there are only ten available copies, the oldest of which was compiled some nine hundred years later than the original.

Over the last fifty years there has been a great deal of research into the whole field of New Testament documentation. There is not space in this book to go into detail as to the methods used, but the research has confirmed that no substantial changes have taken place in the transmission of the texts, and that the Gospels available to us today are accurate.

If you wish to read further on the matter of the historical reliability of the Gospels, there is plenty of material available. I suggest *The New Testament Documents: Are They Reliable?* by F.F. Bruce (IVP 1960). It also contains an extensive reading list on this subject.

The way forward

When we come to the Gospel histories, we can be sure that we have an accurate picture of the Jesus who lived, worked, died and returned to life in Palestine in the first century AD. The God who chose to reveal Himself to us by this method has been kind enough to us to have them preserved for us to read today.

The way forward for you could lie in one of two directions. Firstly, if you are uncertain about whether Jesus is

1. *The New Testament Documents* F.F. Bruce IVP (1960)

really the Son of God, then I think you should go to the Gospels and read them. Luke's is the simplest to read, but Mark is the shortest in length. Why not read all four? As you read them ask yourself the question, Is this person, Jesus mentally deranged? a deceiver? or who He claims to be, the unique Son of God?

Secondly, if you are now convinced that Jesus is the Son of God, then let me encourage you to go on to Part 3 of this book and continue reading, because I want to show you how important it is not to delay but to take action.

Part 3

What's The Alternative?

CHAPTER TEN

What's the Hurry?

If I offer you my friendship I think there are only really
two choices before you. You can reject or accept.

So far I have talked about the very real benefits which
are experienced in life by those who have entered into
relationship with God through Christ. However, the Bible
recognises the possibility of an alternate response — that
of continued rejection. It regards such a response very
seriously and we are warned of its consequences. Some
people are unhappy about this and I am sometimes accused of using scare tactics and of trying to frighten
them. The consequences of continued rebellion to God
are serious *and* frightening.

All the way along the foreshore of one of our bays, the
local councils have erected signs showing a large black
shark and warnings written in several different languages
telling that it is unsafe to swim in the unenclosed sections
of the bay. It would be possible to accuse the council of
engaging in scare tactics. It would be possible to describe
the council's action in terms of restriction of our civil
liberties. But no one would ever dream of doing that
because the danger is real. There is only one way to
describe their action — it is a kind service to people to
warn them of extreme danger. I have noticed though,
that it hasn't stopped people swimming there. I guess you
can't win them all.

Similarly, the Bible warns us of the seriousness of our
danger if we continue to reject God's free offer of pardon
and friendship. It really is a thoughtful loving action on
God's part to warn us. So with that in mind let us look

at what the consequences are and ask what will happen to those who refuse the gospel.

I have delayed using the word hell for as long as possible because it conjures up such strange views in the minds of people. Often the image is that of a person who looks as if he is on his way to a fancy dress ball, a chap with an overgrown toasting fork in his hand, prodding people in the rear end while the flames leap up around them. To the twentieth century mind it is all a bit of a lark.

With a friend I climbed the 463 steps inside the dome of the cathedral in Florence, Italy. The entire ceiling is covered by Vasari's fresco depicting the horrors of the last judgment and hell. There are huge, pink people being chased by dragons and hobgoblins. I must admit that it did seem quaint to me and although my medieval ancestors may have quaked in their boots and been terrified, we were only amused.

About a fortnight later I saw a performance of Mozart's *Don Giovanni,* in which in the last act, Don Giovanni goes to hell. The production was clever but once again, fear was not the emotion I felt. I was quite able to applaud when the curtain came down.

I was discussing the future with a very old man one day and the subject got around to heaven and hell. When he asked if I thought he would go to hell I had to tell him that I certainly did, if he was still unforgiven. He laughed and gave a fairly common reply, "There'll be a lot of my mates there." I think that his view of hell was of an endless pub crawl with no hangover to follow.

Let's have a look at what the Bible says.

Jesus refers to judgment and hell often in His teachings (see Luke 13:5; Mark 9:43). He warns us to be prepared for the judgment day (Luke 21:5-36). However, one of

the most helpful descriptions of judgment is in 2 Thessalonians which was written by the apostle Paul. The little
church in Thessalonica was undergoing heavy persecu-
tion. Paul wrote to tell them that the day when true
justice would come was not then, but that God would
eventually vindicate them.

"All this is evidence that God's judgment is right, and
as a result you will be counted worthy of the kingdom
of God, for which you are suffering. God is just: He
will pay back trouble to those who trouble you and
give relief to you who are troubled, and to us as well.
This will happen when the Lord Jesus is revealed from
heaven in blazing fire with his powerful angels. He will
punish those who do not know God and who do not
obey the Gospel of our Lord Jesus. They will be punished with everlasting destruction and shut out from
the presence of the Lord and from the majesty of his
power on the day he comes to be glorified in his holy
people and to be marvelled at among all those who
have believed" (2 Thessalonians 1:5-10).

It's a fairly stark description.

The basis of the judgment

We have already seen that Jesus will be the agent of the
judgment day since God has given all authority into His
hand (Matthew 28:18; John 5:24-30), and we know why
the judgment day has been delayed. However, we are not
to pretend that it won't happen. So that we can be well
prepared we have been told the basis on which the judgment will be made. "He will punish those who do not
know God and who do not obey the Gospel of our Lord
Jesus."

As a school teacher and a clergyman, during my life I
have both set, and sat for, more examinations than I care
to remember. I know that if one is to pass exams then
nothing is more helpful than to know exactly what questions will be asked.

God has told us exactly what questions we will be asked. Suppose today is the day for me and I find myself in the presence of the Lord Jesus, judge of all the world. The questions are the same for me as for everyone, "John Chapman, did you know God? Did you obey the gospel of the Lord Jesus Christ?"

It appears as though there are two questions but really I see there is only one. I am being asked if I know God personally as opposed to knowing only *about* Him, and the only way I can do that is by responding in obedience to the fact that Jesus is Lord and that He has died for me. It is another way of saying, "Are you really a friend of mine or are you still a rebel?"

Can I say, too, as an old examiner from way back, that I know that no one passes who misreads the question or gives an answer which is not asked for. That is why a good life alone is not sufficient. It would be strange if when Jesus said to me, "John Chapman, did you know God? Did you obey the gospel?", I were to answer, "I've really lived a very decent life. I haven't done anyone any harm. I've been a good neighbour."

"All that is very interesting, John Chapman, irrelevant but interesting, so let me put the question to you again. Did you know God? Did you obey the gospel?"

Being a Christian never was a matter of keeping rules. Rule keeping is so barren. Sometimes when I was teaching, some of the children who never broke the rules (and so could never be punished), made it very clear that they were not my friends nor did they want me as a friend. They kept the rules, but their attitude was that of rebellion.

I read of a couple who had been married for more than twenty years. She had cooked for him, washed, ironed his clothes and mended them, and kept the house spotlessly clean. He had worked hard and had more than provided for them both, yet in the last ten years neither had spoken to the other. Not a very satisfactory relationship I would have thought. Law keeping for its own sake is so hard and barren and not to be compared with the joy of pleasing one you love. Obligatory law keeping is not to be compared to the loving obedience which results from true commitment. So the real question is not, "Did you live a good life?" but "Did you know God by obeying the gospel?" It's all the world of difference.

Lonely life — lonely eternity

The nature of punishment is described in 2 Thessalonians 1:5-10, as extreme loneliness. While I am not frightened by goblins and dragons I am frightened by being lonely. If you're not, it probably means you haven't experienced it. Wait! Paul says, "They will be punished with an everlasting destruction and shut out from the presence of the Lord." What happens is that the punishment fits the crime. If I continue to say to God, "Stay out of my life," then in the end God says, "I will stay out completely."

The term translated as 'eternal destruction' is a difficult one for which to find an easy equivalent in English. It carries the idea of losing everything of value, a total disastrous loss. One day when you have time, make a list of everything in life which really matters to you, the things you really value. Know for a fact that none of these will be in hell. How come? The Bible's view is that every good thing comes from God (James 1:17); loving and caring are gifts from God; friendship and good times come from God, and He has given these gifts indiscriminately to people in His world whether we recognise Him or not. However, when God is rejected, these go with Him. To be God-forsaken is grim in the extreme.

The old man who thinks his mates will be with him in hell is both right and wrong. He's right in thinking they will be there (probably), but he is mistaken in thinking that there will be mateship or friendship there. Friendship exists because God has not left the world He created nor lost interest in it. When I go on saying to God, "Leave me alone", He will say to me, "Very well then, I will leave you *alone.*" Loneliness is the real nature of the punishment.

Hell may be described as rather like watching the news on television. On any night, in almost any country in the world, we are shown, a fire, a bank robbery, armed warfare, an assault victim, etc. Yet, however grim the situation is, someone is trying to make it better. Firemen fight fires; the police are trying to catch the thief; someone is attempting to negotiate a solution to restore world peace; help is available for an assault victim. These people may not be able to solve everything immediately, but at least they are there and represent good opposing evil.

Now imagine an existence where every force which resists evil, and every helpful agency is removed, evil is left to take over, and you have the Bible's picture of hell. Robbery, arson, violence rampant all with no one to help. War with no solution. Just complete and utter loneliness and desolation. No wonder the Bible warns us about it, and urges us to take steps to avoid it.

We cannot fully understand the whole picture, and we are really trying to describe the indescribable.

"He had never felt such aloneness before.

'Where is my wife?' he choked.

Only that awful echo: 'Not here, your wife is not here.'

He tried to piece it all together, but the darkness was too thick. Once in a while he thought he could see a blurred figure or hear an anguished moan.

He remembered the pain — those last moments of terror — but it was nothing compared to the feelings that were creeping into his awareness now. Again he cried:

'Where is my wife?'

'Your wife is not here.'

'Where are my children?'

'Your children are not here.'

He started to grope about in the darkness, but all was blindness.

'My God!' he howled again, 'Let me feel the presence of one single human being!'

"My God" — he hadn't said those words in such a long time. "My God" — and now they seemed so hollow.

Terror was welling up in him. He felt like a small child being threatened by deep darkness. No candles anywhere. No love anywhere. No voice anywhere.

'Where is my wife?' he screamed.

'Your wife is not here.'

'Where are my children?' he pleaded.

'Your children are not here.'

Then the greatest fear of all came to his mind . . . He was terrified to ask but he knew he would have to . . . His whole body trembled as he pursed his lips and wailed into the nebulous night —

'Where . . . oh, where is God!'

As the deepest of all darkness closed in on his soul for all eternity, he heard that hideous echo whispering that most horrifying of all judgments —

'God is not here!"[1]

As I said earlier, some people have objected to the whole idea of judgment and hell. "How can a God of love do that?" is the question. However, it cannot really be any other way.

First, because God takes us and His world seriously. Visiting friends I asked the son of my host how he was getting on at school. He told me that he didn't like school and that his teacher wasn't very interested in him. I immediately went to her defence. "I'm sure you must be mistaken," I said. "I'm sure she is interested in you."

"She isn't," he protested, "she never marks my work." The fact that he was never brought to the test was to him a sure indication that she didn't really care about him.

1. *Like it is Today*, Richard Milham, U.S.A.

Love and wrath are not opposites. Hate is the opposite
to love. It's impossible for them to co-exist, but it is not
the same thing to say love and wrath are incompatible.
Sentimentality is often so lazy that it will not bestir itself.
It just does nothing. But deep genuine love will always
be righteous and angry about anything which is not right.
Only complete carelessness and indifference could cause
God to say "Skip it! It doesn't really matter!"

Second, God must act in judgment or else His entire
plan to rescue His people will be completely ruined again.
The whole show fell apart when mankind turned their
backs on God and placed themselves in a rival position.
God's plan to deal with the situation was to send His Son,
Jesus, in to the world as a reconciling mediator. This He
did through His sinbearing death.

However if everyone is allowed a place in the new
world God has prepared, whether they are friends or
rebels of God, then the whole show will end up exactly
as it was before, and the death of Jesus will have been
for nothing.

To be in a true fellowship with Jesus, the author of
life, is to have life. To refuse the friendship of Jesus is
death, which is separation from Him. It is not possible to
have the benefits of friendship without the commitment
involved.

Three reasons for not delaying
From time to time I talk with people who do believe that
Jesus is the Son of God and they think that sooner or
later they probably will become Christians but they put
off doing anything about it. They don't really give much
thought to it all and 'later' is their theme.

Here are three reasons why you should not delay in
your response to God.
1.   *The brevity of life.* A person ought not to delay because
we never know how long we have to live. There really is
a great uncertainty to life. I have already mentioned the

girl in our congregation with leukaemia. No one would have suspected it a year before. I read in the morning paper of the number of people killed daily on our roads. None of them expected to die. I don't want to be morbid, but I'm trying to be a realist. No one thinks he will be next to die, but it is likely. So the Bible urges each one of us, "Today if you hear his [God's] voice, do not harden your hearts" (Hebrews 4:7). Now is the time to act — not later.

2. *Practice makes perfect.* Every time we put off doing anything about establishing our friendship with God we just get better at putting it off. It is simply a matter of practice. The more regularly we practice the better we become. It is possible that even now as you read this book you've said, "Yes, I've heard it all before." So I want to ask you, "What have you done?"

A fellow clergyman told me of a parishioner whom he visited quite regularly. He had often asked the man to consider the claims of Christ on his life, but the man always made light of it. One day it was discovered that the man had terminal cancer. Again my friend urged him to turn back to Christ for forgiveness. Again he brushed it off carelessly. When he was in the final stages of life and had been lapsing in and out of consciousness, my friend again urged him, pointing out how close he was to death. Regaining consciousness briefly one day, he astounded my friend by saying, "You don't think a strapping bloke like me is about to die, do you?" He died that afternoon. His problem was that he was so well prac-tised in saying "no" that he hardly had to think about it.

3. *Your present position.* It is possible that you may never seriously think about Christianity in the way you are now. If you don't take action now when you are thinking about it, then in the future it will probably seem less serious than it does now when you are so closely examining all the facts. You will be less likely to do anything later, when the investigation is over.

God tells us of His existence so that we can respond to Him in friendship. God sent His Son to die for us. He calls us to come back and warns us not to resist or delay. Now is the time for action.

The question now remains, "What am I supposed to do?" This is detailed in chapter twelve. However, often when I speak to people at this stage they say "But I really *am* a good person. Surely you aren't suggesting that I am in danger, are you?" So before we look at how we are meant to respond to the Lord Jesus we will look at the question, *Why isn't good enough, good enough?*

CHAPTER ELEVEN

Why isn't Good Enough, Good Enough?

One of the most common errors made in thinking about Christianity is to mistake good people for Christians. It is possible to be a good person and be atheist. It is possible to be a good person and be a Buddhist. It is also possible to be a good person and be a Christian. However, having said that, it is necessary to say that it is possible to be good and still go to hell. In fact, hell will be full of good people.

Really good people have several real problems.

Good people are not good enough

The first problem which good people have is that no matter how they try, they can never make themselves good enough for God. It just isn't possible. Jesus tells us what God is like and He then calls on us to be like Him. In the Sermon on the Mount He says, "Be perfect, therefore, as your father in heaven is perfect" (Matthew 5:48).

When an expert on the law asked Jesus what He would have to do to gain eternal life, Jesus asked him, "What is written in the law?" The lawyer answered, "Love the Lord your God with all your heart and with all your soul and with all your strength and with all your mind, and love your neighbour as yourself."

"You have answered correctly," Jesus replied. "Do this and you will live" (Luke 10:27,28). But the real trouble is that none of us can really do that no matter how we try. We just cannot make it. Some people, through a valiant effort, make themselves much better than others. But none of us is really good enough.

Suppose we both decide to go to a concert. When we arrive we discover the tickets cost ten dollars each. We go through our pockets and discover that I have got one dollar and you have eight dollars. You miss the mark by two dollars, but I am much further away than that. Neither of us makes it.

It is exactly the same in the supernatural realm. The real trouble is that we compare ourselves with one another and not with Jesus. If I look around for long enough, ultimately I can usually find someone who appears to be worse than I am. However, I would be foolish to think I am good enough. I need to look at Jesus to see just how far short of the mark I really am, and whether I miss by a little or a lot, I still miss out.

Good people are really too good

The second real problem that good people experience is that they are tempted to believe that they are actually better than they are. From there it is only a very short step to believing that they really *are* good enough for God. Jesus told one of His most penetrating parables about this very thing.

"To some who were confident of their own righteousness and looked down on everybody else, Jesus told this parable: 'Two men went up to the temple to pray, one a Pharisee and the other a tax collector. The Pharisee stood up and prayed about himself: "God, I thank you that I am not like all other men — robbers, evildoers, adulterers — or even like this tax collector. I fast twice a week and give a tenth of all I get.'

But the tax collector stood at a distance. He would not even look up to heaven, but beat his breast and said, 'God, have mercy on me, a sinner.'

I tell you that this man, rather than the other, went home justified before God" (Luke 18:9-14).

If it hadn't come from the lips of Jesus we might be tempted to doubt whether it could be true. The Pharisee really was a good man. He was honest in his business, a good father and a faithful husband. He was even religious into the bargain, but for all that, he was a stranger to God and his 'goodness' actually got in the way of him coming to God for forgiveness. The tax collector was sinful and he knew it, but knowing it was his best asset! He admitted it, threw himself upon God's mercy and was forgiven. He wasn't justified because he was sinful, but because he called on God in trust for mercy. The Pharisee was sinful too, but his 'goodness' blinded him to his need. He was rejected, not because he was good, but because he treated God as if he didn't need Him. The real trouble with being good is we are tempted to think we don't need to be forgiven, well, not much anyway.

Good people are bad news

The real problem with trusting in our own 'goodness' is that we set ourselves completely against God's method of rescuing us. The death and resurrection of Jesus are at the very centre of all God's purposes for His world. So any method which I might devise to get right with God but which bypasses those events, cannot be right. It is possible to be a thoroughly good person and know nothing about Jesus. We could live really good lives today, even if Jesus had not been born or had not died, but when we put our trust in our own goodness we make the message of the gospel, the 'good news', irrelevant. In fact, we treat it as if it were a terrible mistake.

God's plan to rescue us was to send His one and only Son to die for us. Good people say to Him, "You needn't have done that. I don't need it. I'm O.K. the way I am." You see, we are right back to square one again. If we could have made it by being good then there would have been no need for Jesus to die!

Good people confuse us

Good people present us with a problem. A good person's
life is a confusion to us because it seems to be saying,
"Being a Christian is irrelevant. I am a good person and
I'm not a Christian." It is confusing because there is
something quite appealing about good people and other
people are led astray by wanting to be like them. I'm sure
they don't mean to be as dangerous as they are, and
would probably be shocked to hear me say so, but they
are dangerous.

Suppose your next door neighbour on one side is a lazy
good-for-nothing. He regularly comes home drunk, and
just as regularly beats his wife and children. No one will
want to pattern their lives on him. Just for argument's
sake let us suppose on the other side your neighbour is
kind and thoughtful, generous and understanding. He
comes to offer help when you are in need even before
you ask and nothing seems to be a bother to him. You
will describe him as "the salt of the earth". You will hold
him up as an example to your children, "I hope when
you grow up you will be like Mr. Snooks." Yet if Snooks
is not in a personal relationship with God, he is likely to
"con" us into believing that life with Christ doesn't really
matter much. He may not mean to but he will.

Others can confuse too

Confusing as these good people are, they are not the only
ones who confuse. I am sure we have all been confused
by people who claim to be Christian and yet do not behave as if they are. They talk about Jesus yet do not live
like Him. They are very confusing. My father was cheated
in a business deal by someone who was a 'church' man.
Dad was rightly browned off by that, and said to me, "Do
you want me to become like that man?"

"I wish you were both like Jesus," was my reply. But I
know how he felt. You may have been hurt or confused

by some people. Try not to let them put you off. Look back to Jesus, He is not a bit confusing.

Jesus is not against being good

True Christians who have genuinely surrendered their lives to Christ in commitment and trust should be growing daily more and more like Jesus. They should be getting better. Some of them you might describe as 'good'. If you asked them why they were trying to live a good life, they would say, "I am so thankful to Jesus for dying for me and for my forgiven sins that I am living my life in a way which says to Him, 'thank you'."

If you asked them the question, "Do you think God will allow you into heaven because you have lived a good life?" they would answer, "No! God will allow me into heaven because Christ has died for me. I have asked God to have mercy on me and to forgive me and because of Jesus I know He will."

They are the best examples. If you have met someone like that you are most fortunate. However, don't be discouraged if you haven't. Jesus is still real and very appealing.

Christians *should* be good people. If you asked them, "Do you try to live a good life to win God's favour?". "No", they would answer, "I don't need to win God's favour. Christ has done that for me already and because of Him God accepts me."

"Why do you try to live a good life then?"

"Because I know God likes it, so I do it to show my gratitude to Him for receiving me and making me His own."

There is a real difference between the person who lives the good life in the hope of *winning* God's favour and the person who lives a good life because he knows he already *has* God's favour. It may be subtle but there really is an enormous difference.

Good people think they are better than God

The trouble with really good people who aren't Christians is that they rewrite, what God has said. He says, "You can't make it on your own."

They say, "I can make it on my own."

God says, "Be perfect."

They say, "Be the best you can."

God says, "Repent."

They say, "I'm good enough as I am."

God says, "You are only acceptable to me because of the death of my Son."

They say, "My life is acceptable as it is."

God says, "You need forgiveness."

They say, "Look at my goodness."

In the end if I hope that I will be O.K. because of the good life I lead I am setting myself up as better than God.

Good people only fool themselves

John says some helpful words for us all. "If we claim to be without sin, we deceive ourselves and the truth is not in us" (1 John 1:8). Nothing is so pathetic as to be self deceived. If I think I'm good enough without Christ, then who will be deceived? God? No way! Will others who know me, be deceived? No way! They know my short-comings only too well. I will be the only one deceived.

John gives the solution to my problem, "If we confess our sins, he [God] is faithful and just and will forgive us our sins and purify us from all unrighteousness" (1 John 1:9).

Part 4

What's To Be Done?

CHAPTER TWELVE

What am I Supposed to do?

Well, what does a person do to become a Christian?

God has acted on our behalf. He has sent His Son to die and rise again. He has sent His Spirit to warn us of judgment and to teach us the true meaning of Jesus' work for us. There only remains for us to respond positively to God's offer of friendship and pardon.

Becoming a Christian is much more like getting married than it is like catching the mumps. You know what it is like with the mumps. You wake up one morning and it has crept up on you unawares. Your face and neck are swollen and you feel awful. Marriage on the other hand is nothing like that at all. If you wake up one morning and discover you're not the only one there it would never occur to you to say, "Fancy that, I'm married!" With mumps we have very little to do, whereas marriage is achieved by taking action and making decisions.

I remember well the marriage I performed between Paul and Jane. We had spoken together many times about what they were doing, but then the day actually came, and Paul and Jane were both standing before me. I addressed Paul, "Will you have this woman for your lawful wedded wife?" Notice I didn't say, "How do you feel towards this woman?" I wouldn't have run the risk, I knew how he felt. He was terribly nervous. During the few minutes we stood in the church before Jane came, he put his handkerchief into at least four different pockets and each time he looked for it he couldn't find it. I didn't even ask him if he loved her, (although I'm sure that it is a great help in marriage!) I asked Paul to exercise his will, not his emotions. I said, "Will you have this woman for your wife, to have and to hold from this day forward, for better, for worse, for richer or poorer, in sickness and in health, and forsaking all other cleave only to her [the conditions of his intention] so long as you both shall live [the extent of his intention]."

To which he answered, "I will." Having clearly established what he intended to *do,* I moved to Jane and asked her the same, to which she answered, "I will." It was on the basis of their declared intention that I then pronounced that they were man and wife.

Becoming a Christian is much more like that than it is like catching the mumps. You don't wake up one morning and say, "I think I've become a Christian." You *do* something with your *will.* God has declared His intentions towards us. I have listed them in chapter five. It is now up to us to clearly make up our minds and decide what action we will take.

So often people delay in becoming Christians because they are expecting some mystical experience which someone has described to them. They know that what they are doing is supernatural so they think it is more likely to be an emotional response or one of 'gut' reaction rather than one of the will. It isn't really like that. So many have made false starts without thinking it through and then in the cold light of day whatever decision they had made, dwindled away and amounted to nothing.

As with marriage, emotions may be involved and in most cases will be, but they are not the essence of the action. I think this is why so many people are confused when I ask the simple question, "Are you a Christian?" I get the strangest assortment of answers.

"I'm not really sure."

Some say, "I hope so!"

Others yet say, "I don't know if you can ever know." It's an interesting thing but when I ask people, "Are you married?", I have never once had an indefinite reply!

It's either "Yes" or "No" or "I used to be."

So how do I say, "I will" to the Lord Jesus Christ and enter into a new life with Him.

Do you remember that I began this book by describing the ways we try to relate to God? We either ignore Him, or use Him, or we just react in open hostility. I have tried to show that each of these constitutes in one form or another, an attitude of rebellion. Well, what needs to happen? Suppose I have been introduced to you and in our first encounter I am appallingly rude to you. When we meet on the next occasion it's no good my pretending that we haven't met, or that I haven't been rude. If I want to have you as a friend I must take action to rectify the damage my stupidity has caused. An apology is in order. So I throw myself on your mercy, "I'm so glad I've met you again. When we met last I was terribly rude to you. I wonder if you can find it in your heart to forgive me? I'd really like to have you as a friend. I can't imagine what came over me." The ball is now in your court. You, and you alone, must decide whether there is any hope for friendship.

It is very similar with God. We need to come back and make our apologies and state our intentions for the future and throw ourselves upon His mercy. In the Bible this action is called repentance.

Repentance — what it is
Preaching, in the Bible, is directed towards repentance. John the Baptist began his ministry by saying, "Repent, because the kingdom of heaven is near" (Matthew 3:2). This was also the way Jesus began His preaching ministry (Matthew 4:17) and He continued throughout His ministry on this theme (Luke 13:5).

The preaching of the apostles was directed towards the action of repentance.

"Repent and be baptised, everyone of you in the name of Jesus Christ so that your sins may be forgiven" (Acts 2:38) was the call by the apostle Peter on the day of Pentecost, and it was a theme of Paul's preaching.

"In the past God overlooked such ignorance but now he commands all people everywhere to repent" (Acts

17:30) Paul said to the Athenians. In fact, this appeal was always present in his ministry. He described his ministry to the church leaders at Ephesus in these terms: "You know that I have not hesitated to preach anything that would be helpful to you but have taught you publicly and from house to house. I have declared to both Jews and Greeks that they must turn to God in repentance and have faith in our Lord Jesus" (Acts 20:21). This is a very important statement because it contains in a summary form our response, repentance toward God and faith in the Lord Jesus Christ.

In essence, repentance is a change of mind towards God with an accompanying change of behaviour. It is the point at which I admit that I have rebelled against God's rightful rule over my life and I declare my intention to obey God in the future to the best of my ability.

A genuine repentance would require that where my rebellion against God had involved other people as well then I would need to make restitution whenever that was possible. This is illustrated for us in the behaviour of the tax collector, Zacchaeus, who became a disciple of Jesus. In the presence of his friends and Jesus, he stated, "Lord! Here and now I give half of my possessions to the poor, and if I have cheated anybody out of anything, I will pay back four times the amount" (Luke 19:8).

He recognised that Jesus was his Lord. His new life was marked by a new generosity and he would make good, with interest, those he had cheated. Because we are all different, the way we demonstrate our repentance will vary according to people and circumstances. Toward God it will be the same; we acknowledge our sin and we turn back to serve Jesus as our Lord.

I visited a young man who was converted at an open-air meeting. Some Christians were telling the Gospel in the main street, and he heard about God's action towards him in sending Jesus to die so that all people could be forgiven. In his heart he responded in true repentance and acknowledged Jesus as his Lord, but he had a real problem. For the previous four years he had been regularly 'earning' his living by breaking and entering. For him repentance meant going to the local police station and giving himself up. We met him in Long Bay Gaol.

For a small girl at a Sunday School camp, repentance took a totally different turn. She told me she wanted to repent and acknowledge Jesus as her Lord. "What difference do you think that will make to the way you behave at home?" I asked.

"Well, one of my jobs is to make jelly for lunch on Sunday. I never really mix it until all the crystals dissolve, but now I know I will have to," she replied. I must confess that mixing the jelly crystals has not been part of my repentance, but I don't doubt there will be a real expression of repentance and a change in your life as there has been in others.

When various people came to John the Baptist to ask how repentance should affect their lives, he gave various answers. To the crowd he said, "The man with two tunics should share with him who has none, and the one who has food should do the same" (Luke 3:11). To the tax collectors, "Don't collect any more than you are required to" (Luke 3:12). To the soldiers, "Don't extort money and don't accuse people falsely — be content with your pay" (Luke 3:14). A timely word for workers today.

For the rich young ruler who wanted eternal life and came to Jesus seeking it, repentance meant giving his money away to the poor. He baulked at that, for we read that "he went away sad, because he had great wealth" (Matthew 19:16-22).

For the woman at the well in Samaria, it meant dealing with serious moral and marital problems. In acknowledgment of Jesus as Messiah she went off to bring others to "see the man who told me everything I ever did". She did not baulk at the public acknowledgment of her sin. (John 4:4-30).

I cannot say what result will follow true repentance for you. You may end up in gaol. You may have to beat the jelly crystals until they all dissolve. But God will know and His way will be for your welfare, so when you repent ask Him to help you to remember where you should make restitution.

Many years ago I counselled a young lady at a convention. She was converted and turned to Jesus as her new Lord. She told me her tale. For the previous six months she had been paid compensation by the firm which employed her, a pastoral company. She had tried to commit suicide by taking poison. However, when admitted to hospital she had claimed that she had been bitten by a snake while working. She had been off work ever since. She asked me what repentance would mean. Well it was obvious that she would have to stop taking money from her employers and make some effort to repay them. I put her in touch with a Christian lawyer who immediately began to negotiate with the company. They stopped paying her and she made an offer to repay them over a period of time. The company had a real problem. No one had ever done that before and they had no mechanism to deal with it. In the end they found it easier to deal with the problem by waiving the debt. She was very fortunate. It may be like that with you. It may be like the boy in Long Bay Gaol. I'm not God, I don't know.

Before I leave this, I don't want to imply that repentance is primarily centred upon our fellow men. Repentance primarily involves our attitude toward God as our God. From it flows new, right behaviour. Wrong behaviour in whatever form it takes, is always and from the beginning, against God.

David, an ancient king of Israel and one of God's people, sinned very greatly. He lusted after another man's wife, committed adultery, lied to her husband and when she became pregnant, he even engineered the murder of her husband in an effort to try and 'hush up' the whole affair. It was a terribly sordid affair. David may have got away with it but God confronted him through the prophet Nathan (2 Samuel 12:1-14). David repented and you can read his response in Psalm 51. In it he makes this statement, "Against you . . . have I sinned and done what is evil in your sight" (Psalm 51:4). He had also sinned against the woman and her husband and all God's people. But he was right in seeing his sin to be primarily against God.

Repentance is a change of mind and will towards God. I say, *"Lord God, I have rebelled against you in the past. I have not wanted Jesus to rule over me as Lord. Please forgive me. My intention for the future is to serve Him to the best of my ability. Please help to to do this."*

This is the first part of a true commitment to Christ.

Repentance — what it is not

Repentance is not basically feeling sorry. This is such a common mistake that it is worth spending a moment to comment on it. Some of our sins make us feel bad. Others leave us fairly unaffected. Some make us feel guilty, others hardly cause a ripple across our pond. You may feel really sorry about something you have done, but have no real desire to start living a new life under Christ's authority. You may feel a strong sense of relief when something which has really been bothering you moves on. That is not repentance. It is possible to experience real sorrow and not be repentant. On the other hand you can be truly repentant and not feel sorry.

1. You can be sorrowful and not be repentant. In repentance the question is not "Are you sorry?", but "Why are you sorry?" Is it because you feel bad or because you have sinned against God and have turned your back on Him.

I have met so many people who appeared to start so well as Christians but who in a few years had given it all away. In almost every case I know of, it was because they had never really repented. They had had problems and they rushed to God to solve them. When the problem went so did their 'Christianity'. It was not based on the fact that they had surrendered their will permanently to Jesus the Lord. Like marriage, repentance begins with commitment, and like marriage, it takes a lifetime for it to work out in practice. A repentant attitude towards God continues throughout the whole of a Christian's life. The way you begin is the way you are to continue. "As you received Christ Jesus as Lord," Paul says to the Colossians, "continue to live in him" (Colossians 2:6).

2. *You can be repentant and not sorrowful.* Jesus tells the story about a farmer and his two sons — "What do you think? There was a man who had two sons. He went to the first and said, 'Son, go and work today in the vineyard.'

'I will not,' he answered, but later changed his mind [repented] and went.

Then the father went to the other son and said the same thing.

He answered, 'I will, sir,' but he did not go.

Which of the two did what his father wanted?" (Matthew 21:28-32).

You can imagine the situation. The father comes to the first son, "Go work in the vineyard," he says.

Whether in his mind or out aloud you can hear the son say, "I'm sick of this place, I'm sick of the farm and I'm sick of work! I'm not going." He doesn't like it. But finally he repents and the reason we know that he did repent was that he went to work. I dare say he didn't like the farm or the farm work any more when he went, than when he said that he wouldn't go. But he did change his mind and exercised his will and obeyed. The second boy was full of good feelings toward his father but he was no real son, he said one thing and meant another. He changed his mind and exercised his will and disobeyed.

Will God have us back?
Two boys ran away from home. One was ten years old and the other only seven. They had had a disagreement

with their father and they decided to 'run away'. They hid in a cave near a river at the back of their home and stayed there until it grew dark. They then decided to go back home, having taught their father a big enough lesson. When he saw them coming around the corner of the house the father swept them up in his arms and said, "Hullo, you two. Great to have you back home again. I thought you'd left, but I'm so glad you haven't. Come and have some tea."

I was telling this story one night at a dinner for teenagers. One of them said to me afterwards, "They were lucky. My old man half killed me when I came home."

The question is: Suppose I do come back to God and truly repent. I confess that I have rebelled against Him and I declare my intention to try to live under Jesus' Lordship. I throw myself on God's mercy and say, "Can you find it in your heart to forgive me?" Will he have me back?

God's answer is: "Because my Son, Jesus Christ, has died for you, I will forgive you and take you back as a true friend. You had better believe it!" (see 1 John 1:7,9; Romans 5:1; 2 Corinthians 5:21).

"Believing it" is the other aspect of a genuine response toward God. Can I remind you how Paul described his own ministry, "I have declared to both Jews and Greeks that they must turn to God in repentance and have faith in our Lord Jesus Christ" (Acts 20:21).

Faith — what it is

Faith is really trusting God, believing He will keep His word. In the Bible, Abraham is held up to us as an example of the man of faith. God made him a promise and although it was years and years before he received what had been promised, Abraham continued to trust God. He knew that God was reliable and would keep His word. As time went by it became more and more difficult for the promise to be kept. Abraham did not waver. He knew God could be trusted. (You can read his story in Genesis chapters 12 to 21 and Paul's comments on him in Romans 4:18-25).

The best definition of faith I have been able to find in the Bible is in Romans 4:21. Paul says of Abraham that he was "fully persuaded that God had power to do what he had promised."

To put our faith in the Lord Jesus means that we believe that He died and rose for us so we can be forgiven (Romans 4:25) and that God will receive us because of Jesus. We believe it because God says so.

Earlier we saw how the death of Jesus causes us to be right with God. He rescues us from the consequences of our rebellion. However, the death of Jesus does not rescue everybody in the world. Only those who trust Him.

The person who puts his faith in what Jesus has done for him must abandon the trust he formerly had in himself. He may have thought he was quite a good person and that he was perfectly acceptable to God. Now he realises that he is only acceptable to God because of Jesus. He transfers his trust. He was mistaken (or wilful) in believing in himself. He is not mistaken in putting his confidence in Christ Jesus.

Here is a question for you. The answer to it will show exactly where your trust is placed.

Question: "If you were to die today and stood in the presence of God and He said to you, 'Why should I let you into my heaven?' what would you answer?"

If your answer begins "Because I. . .", then your trust is placed in yourself.

The true Christian who has responded in repentance and faith would answer, "Because Jesus died and rose again for me." Such a person's confidence and trust is in Jesus.

Faith — what it is not
I find that there is even more confusion about what faith is than there is about the nature of repentance.

1. *Faith is not feeling.* When people say to me, "I wish I had your faith", I get the impression that they are looking for an emotional experience which will cause them to have faith. They are thinking about faith as a mystical 'something' which happens to some people. If you have it, it's good luck; if you haven't, it's bad luck and there isn't much you can do about it. They feel as if it might be 'caught' by performing some religious ritual or being in some 'holy' place. It isn't that at all. When people say, "I wish I had your faith", I reply, "You have as much faith as I have. You've just aimed it in a different direction."

Outside my home I board a bus to take me to the railway station. Because I can never remember when they run at weekends, I need to look up the time-table. I exercise faith in the bus company that the bus will come when they say so. Consequently I get ready to go. I could exercise the same faith and direct it towards my ability to remember when the buses run. Instead of looking up the time-table I could guess, get ready and go to the bus stop. In my case the latter is less reliable than the former. Not because I have more faith on either occasion, but because my faith is used on a more reliable piece of information. The bus time-table is more reliable than my memory. So the time-table is a better thing to put my trust in than is my memory.

One day I misread the time-table and went to get the bus. Of course it didn't come, although I had complete faith that it would, my faith didn't bring the bus, not because I didn't have enough, but because I was mistaken in the way I used my faith.

Faith, like repentance, is something we do with our wills. We know that God is trustworthy. He will do what He says, so we place our confidence in Him. We trust Him.

2. *Faith is not only intellectual assent.* Faith is more than such simple intellectual assent as when someone might

say, "I believe Canberra is the capital of Australia". Many people who believe in God still resist Him and do not repent. Some people who actually believe that Jesus died so that their sins might be forgiven do not come to Him in repentance and trust. James tells us that demons believe in God and tremble (James 2:19).

3.   *Faith is not blind hope or wishful thinking.* Some people have described faith as the thing you do when all the known information has run out. They say, "There can't be any evidence for that, you must believe it by faith". That is not the Bible perspective at all.

Others tell me that if I believe something strongly enough then God is bound to do it. I think this is wishful thinking and not faith and can lead to the terrible presumption of trying to manipulate God through our prayers. God is His own person. He does what He promises to do. If He has made no promise in a given area we will just have to trust Him to do what is loving and right, because He is that kind of a person.

4.   *Faith is not trusting in faith.* 'Believing' is neither good nor bad. It is neutral. It's not *that* I believe, but *in whom* I believe. Suppose I come into a room dragging an electric light cord. At the end are two bare wires. "Hold them," I say, "the power is not turned on." You may believe me but that belief will not be worth a cent if I'm lying. Your faith is *good*, but it is totally misplaced. There is nothing wrong with your faith. I'm the one who is wrong. You should never have trusted me.

When the Bible speaks of faith it is always talking of the *object* of faith, the Lord Jesus, rather than the activity of faith. It really worries me to hear people say, "I know God will receive me because of my faith." Their faith in whom? For their faith is still directed to themselves. They have 'faith in faith'.

It is time now for action

Well, where are we now? We have spoken about our need to be rescued from ourselves and the mess to which our rebellion has brought us.

We have spoken about what God has done for us in sending Jesus into the world to live and die for us so that we can be forgiven. What more is God supposed to do?

He does more. He warns us of the danger of refusing to come back or of delaying. He may have provided you with a Christian friend who lent you this book and reading it has given you yet more time to consider what God has done. What more is God supposed to do?

He does more. He continues to reassure us of the benefits of friendship with Him. He promises His commitment to us. Isn't it time you committed yourself to Him in repentance and faith?

You may have reached this position before and somehow you didn't exercise your will and say, "I will." It may be the first time you've thought about it. However, whether it's 'old' or 'new', it really is time for action.

You might like to pray this prayer of repentance and faith or make up one for yourself. The words alone do not matter so much as being repentant and trusting Jesus.

"O God, I want to confess to you that I have rebelled against you in my thinking, in my speaking and in my actions. I'm sorry I have acted like that. From today onward I will serve Jesus as my Lord to the best of my ability. Please help me to do that. Lord Jesus, thank you for dying and rising again for me that my sins might be forgiven. Please forgive me and cleanse me from all my sins and give me the gift of eternal life. Please come to me and take full control of my life. Amen."

If you have prayed this prayer or a similar one, you can be sure that God has heard it and *answered* it. You have been forgiven, cleansed and you are acceptable to God. I am overjoyed for you. Welcome to God's people! You have just begun a new and exciting life in friendship with the living God.

But you are a beginner and as such you need help. Two things remain to be done. First, you need to know what to do in order to grow up and mature as a Christian and, second, you need to be sure that what you have done really has worked. These are the subjects of the next two chapters.

However, before we leave this chapter, a final word.

Both repentance and faith are gifts from God
Both repentance and faith are gifts which come from God (Acts 11:18; Philippians 1:29). If you find you want to become a Christian and you cannot repent and trust God, you should beg God to have mercy on you and to give you these gifts and you should continue to pray for them until He gives them to you. You can be sure God will not mock you, He will answer your prayer.

If you have turned to God in repentance and faith, why don't you stop right now and thank God for giving you these gifts?

CHAPTER THIRTEEN

Can I be Sure?

The first time that I went overseas was to visit India. One of the many things which needed to be done before I left was vaccination against smallpox. In time I presented myself to my local doctor who duly did his stuff and said, "Come back in three weeks and we'll see if it has taken". Well, I did go back but there was really no need. It had taken alright. Day and night my entire arm bore witness to the fact that it had truly worked.

Sometimes in the early stages of the Christian life we find ourselves wondering whether or not we might have fooled ourselves when we became Christians. We become uncertain about whether it has really taken or not. So before this book comes to an end I want to answer the question — "Can I really be sure I am a Christian?"

A terrible presumption

Several years ago a famous pianist toured Australia. It was the practice at the Australian Broadcasting Commission to ask guest artists to sign the Visitors' Book and to include an identifying title. He said, "But what will I write?" Someone suggested, "The greatest living pianist". He smiled, picked up the pen, wrote, then closed the book. Later when it was opened they discovered after his name the modest caption, 'piano player!' Such humility is always appealing. Sometimes a person feels ill at ease about calling oneself a Christian. Some feel that it might be presumptuous and that something less definite might be helpful.

However the Bible wants us, not only to be Christian, but to know for certain that we are. John wrote a letter to some first century Christians in which he said, "I write these things to you who believe in the name of the Son of God so that you may know that you have eternal life" (1 John 5:13). He wanted them to be certain; and that book would be a very good one to read when you may feel uncertain.

Paul, the apostle, was able to say as the end of his life approached, "The time has come for my departure. I have fought the good fight, I have finished the race, I have kept the faith. Now there is in store for me the crown of righteousness, which the Lord, the righteous Judge, will award to me on that day — and not only to me, but also to all who have longed for his appearing" (2 Timothy 4:6-8). Not only was he sure about his future, but he still extends that certainty to all who have longed for Jesus' appearing.

When Paul wrote to the Philippian church he expressed certainty about them and their standing as Christians ". . . being confident of this [very thing]," he said, "that he who began a good work in you will carry it on to completion until the day of Christ Jesus" (Philippians 1:6). This confidence was in God, not in the Christians at Philippi. Paul knew that the God who had started something was well able to finish it. It is not a presumption to be sure that we are Christians, neither is it a lack of humility. Indeed to do the opposite is a presumption. To be uncertain when God says we are truly His, is to upstage God again. That is a terrible presumption.

That roller coaster feeling

I was converted at the age of seventeen. I didn't know much about the Bible and I wasn't really helped very much in the church I attended. On the night I was converted I experienced an immense feeling of relief at the thought of my sins being forgiven and that God would receive me. In fact, I felt great! Of course that feeling didn't last, but it presented me with a problem which went unresolved for a couple of years. I thought that the great feeling was really the Holy Spirit dwelling inside me. I was mistaken. When the feeling began to dwindle and I returned to normal, I started to panic, "Where has the Holy Spirit gone?" At church on any Sunday night I was usually able to get the feeling back again. I was re-charged! But, although the batteries were great on Sunday night, they were not long lasting and by Wednesday or Thursday I was at the bottom of that low trough. I survived until Sunday when I would soar to the top of the roller coaster again. Up-down-up-down I went. My feelings were not very reliable. Someone said to me recently, "Your feelings have more to do with the condition of your liver than they do with the condition of your soul." I've found that very helpful. My trouble in those early days was that I had wrong expectations and I was trusting in the wrong things.

So how can we be sure? In a nutshell — we can be sure because of God. Who He is, what He said and what He has done. If it depended upon us we would be full of uncertainty because we are unreliable. But because it depends upon God, there need be no uncertainty.

1. God has spoken
God has spoken and when He does so things begin to happen. When God says something, you can be sure that it is so.

a) God has spoken about the Lord Jesus. God tells us that He will receive us and forgive us because of Jesus. The Bible is full of promises to this effect.

"We accept man's testimony, but God's testimony is greater because it is the testimony of God which he has given about His Son. Anyone who believes in the Son of God has this testimony in his heart. Anyone who does not believe God has made him out to be a liar, because he has not believed the testimony God has given about His Son. And this is the testimony: God has given us eternal life, and this life is in his Son. He who has the Son has life; he who does not have the Son of God does not have life" (1 John 5:9-12).

You can be sure from God's point of view that if you have believed in the Lord Jesus Christ you have eternal life.

Listen to this promise, "If we walk in the light, as he is in the light, we have fellowship with one another, and the blood of Jesus, his Son, purifies us from every sin" (1 John 1:7). John tells us here that the death of Jesus [blood of Jesus] is such that it continually cleanses us from every sin, even the last one. So know for a fact if you are in Christ you have been cleansed from every sin. God says that you will be treated as if you had never sinned.

Paul asks the question, "Who will bring any charge against those whom God has chosen?" (Romans 8:33). It's a good question too! Imagine you are in the presence of God on judgment day and someone says, "Does anyone have anything against this person?" You would normally quake in your boots at such a prospect. You know there are many. Yet God says, "Silence — don't speak anyone. I have justified this person."

"It is God who justifies" (Romans 8:33).

Because the life and work of Jesus is so completely acceptable to God, you and I can be completely acceptable also. It is as if when we turned to the Lord Jesus in repentance and faith we were given two certificates. On the first one it reads: 'This is to certify that the bearer has lived a perfect life'. On the other it says: 'This is to certify that the bearer has paid the full penalty of all sins'.

If on the day of judgment you were to produce them, either would stand you in good stead. With both you will be completely secure. If someone says, "Wherever did you get them?" You will be able to say, "They are gifts, and given to me by the Lord Jesus."

They will no doubt say, "That's right, He did live a perfect life and He did pay the penalty for all sins. He and only He is able to give you such a gift."

In case you think this is an exaggeration, hear what God says, "the gift of God is eternal life in Jesus Christ our Lord" (Romans 6:23).

If it depended on us and what we had done we would be full of uncertainty, but God has spoken about Jesus. It really depends on Him.

b)   *God has spoken about our sins.* From time to time I am reminded of things I have done in the past and which, so far as I am aware, no one else knows about; things for which I am very ashamed; things which I'd rather others didn't know about. When I am reminded I often feel as if I am unforgiven. It is as if my guilty conscience comes back to life and just won't lie down.

I met a lady at a convention who told me that God had revealed to her that if she committed a certain sin again, (she didn't tell me what it was) she would never be able to be forgiven. Well you know where that idea comes from! You can smell the sulphur fumes all over it. It came straight from the 'pit'.

This accusing spirit is none other than the work of the devil himself. He is called the "accuser of our brothers" (Revelation 12:10), and "the father of lies" (John 8:44) and his sole aim is to so discourage us that we doubt our standing before God.

What does God say about our sins?

Psalm 103:11,12
"For as high as the heavens are above the earth, so great is his love for those who fear him; as far as the east is from the west, so far has he removed our transgressions from us."

Isaiah 38:17
"You have put all my sins behind your back."

Micah 7:19

"You will again have compassion on us; you will tread
our sins underfoot and will hurl all our iniquities into
the depths of the sea."

Isaiah 43:25

"I, even I, am he who blots out your transgressions,
for my own sake, and remembers your sins no more."

In a poetic way God says that our sins are gone as far
as the east is from the west; in the bottom of the sea;
behind His back; trampled under foot; blotted out from
His memory.

Sometimes when you apologise after an argument people say, "I'd forgotten all about it." However, when things
get rough again you discover they haven't forgotten about
it at all. They bring it up again!

You can be certain God will never bring up your past.
It has been dealt with completely. You can be sure of
that.

c) *God has spoken about prayer.* There are some conditions
which God makes about prayer and which if we fulfil
them, He will positively give us what we asked for.

"This is the assurance we have in approaching God:
that if we ask anything *according to his will,* he hears us.
And if we know that he hears us — whatever we ask —
we know that we have what we asked of him" (1 John
5:14-15).

Jesus said, "I tell you the truth, my Father will give
you whatever you ask *in my name*" (John 16.23).

The condition for receiving what we ask is that we do
it "according to God's will" and "in the name of Jesus",
which means according to the character of Jesus.

We know that God longs that all people will be saved
(1 Timothy 2:4). We know that Jesus came to seek and
to save the lost (Luke 19:10). So you can be certain that
if you prayed the prayer at the end of chapter twelve, or

a similar one, then God has given you what you asked for. It would be good to go back and read again just what you did ask God to do for you.

Our feelings may play tricks with us but the fact remains that *God has spoken*. So when my feelings are inaccurate, they are to be ignored. When they are correct, they are to be enjoyed.

2. God has acted
Not only has God spoken but He has acted on our behalf.

a) God has acted in history. Sometimes in our lives things happen which cause us to wonder whether in fact God does love us. It might be the death of a loved one, or circumstances much worse. There may have been some terrible disaster which made us feel that God turned His back on us. How can I believe in God in such times as those? Because God has acted in history, and showed us His love in such an unmistakable way that it cannot be changed by our circumstances no matter how bad they may seem to be.

In Jerusalem in the first century God sent His one and only Son into the world. It really did happen. His mother was Mary. He did "go about doing good and healing all who were under the power of the devil, because God was with Him" (Acts 10:38). He did take the punishment which our sins deserved and He did rise again so we could know. If we had been there in the upper room with the disciples when Jesus appeared, we like Thomas, could have touched Jesus to be sure that we weren't dreaming. It happened. God demonstrated in history how much He loves us. "For God so loved the world that he gave his one and only Son, that whoever believes in him shall not perish but have eternal life" (John 3:16). Nothing which subsequently happens can change that. We vary within ourselves, the past does not. That is why we can be sure.

From time to time I wake up and feel as if I can't be bothered being a Christian any more. I don't want to read the Bible. I don't want to pray and I'm sick of trying to be kind to people. I feel like 'chucking it all in'. What stops me? I sit on the side of my bed and ask myself the following questions: "Did you receive some new historical information which shows that Jesus didn't die and rise again from the dead?" Answer: No!

"Did Jesus go back to heaven?" — Yes.

"Is He coming back again?" — Yes.

Well, John Chapman, it doesn't seem as if you have much room for manoeuvring. Get up and get on with it. I have found it very sustaining. *God has acted* for me.

b)   *God has acted in our lives.* Not only has God acted for us but He has also acted *in us*. We became Christians because of the Holy Spirit whom God sent to work with and in us.

I had some surgery done only once. I was given some drug which placed me in a wonderful state of euphoria. I was wheeled into an operating theatre and my surgeon wished me the time of day and that's all I remember. In what seemed like a split second, but which was I suppose about an hour, my surgeon was gently slapping my face and saying, "It's all over now, old man."

"All over?" It seemed as if it had hardly begun. It was nothing. Within two hours I knew it had happened. Those of you who have undergone surgery know what I mean, those of you who haven't are lucky. For weeks afterward I knew that the operation had taken place. Today I still have the unmistakeable proof of that operation although the evidence is less spectacular than it was in those far off days. The Holy Spirit's work is very much like that. We recognise it much more by the results which flow from it than we do while He is at work.

Jesus describes the Spirit's work as being like the wind which blows and you see the result of it by trees moving but you don't know where it comes from or where it goes to (John 3:8).

Well, what are these results?

A new attitude towards Jesus

It is the work of the Holy Spirit to teach us about Jesus and convince us that He is Lord (John 16:8-11). This is one of the reasons why we are hardly ever conscious of the Holy Spirit Himself because He is always drawing our attention to the Lord Jesus. The more He does His work the more conscious of Jesus we become. Paul told the Christians at Corinth that "no-one can say, 'Jesus is Lord', except by the Holy Spirit" (1 Corinthians 12:3). Before we became Christians we may have given assent in some vague way that Jesus was God's Son, but we had no intention of letting Him run our lives. When we became Christians we said that we wanted to truly acknowledge Jesus as our Lord. We wanted Him to rule over us as Master. We did that because of the Holy Spirit whom God had given to us.

A new attitude towards sin

Before we became Christians we didn't worry about our sins against God unless there were repercussions. We didn't bother about the fact that they were offensive to God and had created a real barrier between us and God. But what is the position now? Our sins do worry us. We are making a genuine effort to turn away from them. We wish we were better at it than we are. Sometimes we get discouraged because we aren't managing any better. Paul expressed how we all feel from time to time when he said, "I have a desire to do what is good, but I cannot carry it out. For what I do is not the good I want to do; no, the evil I do not want to do, this I keep on doing" (Romans 7:18b,19). This certainly is not the attitude of an unbeliever. When we were non-Christians we would have said — "I have a desire to do what I like and what's more, I do it." This change has been brought about by the work of the Holy Spirit.

John described it like this, "No-one who lives in Him keeps on sinning. No-one who continues to sin has either seen him or known him . . .No-one who is born of God will continue to sin, because God's seed remains in him, he cannot go on sinning, because he has been born of God" (1 John 3:6,9).

These verses are a bit of a shock when you first read them. It doesn't mean that Christians are perfect and never commit any sins ever again. John, in this letter, defined sin as "lawlessness" (1 John 3:4), which is exactly what we were like before we became Christians. We had no intention of obeying God. That has gone. If you re-state the above passage, you will see it is very reassuring, "No one who continues in lawlessness has either seen him or known him. . .No one born of God will continue in lawlessness because God's seed remains in him; he cannot go on in lawlessness because he has been born of God."

From time to time we do commit acts of sin but because we are God's children we quickly repent, confess them and know we have been forgiven (1 John 1:9). We do not, however, continue in unbridled lawlessness. John uses two expressions which describe the work of the Holy Spirit. He says we have been "born of God" and "God's seed remains in us". It is because we have been "born from above" or "born of the Spirit" (John 3:8) that we have this new attitude towards sin. It is another tell-tale mark that the Holy Spirit is at work in our lives. All Christians have it.

A new attitude towards God's people

Another work of the Holy Spirit which reassures us that we are God's children is a new love which we have for God's people. God calls on us to do it and we respond by trying to do so. "Dear friends, since God so loved us, we ought to love one another. No-one has ever seen God; but if we love each other, God lives in us" (1 John 4:11,12), is how John put it. If you weren't a Christian you would not bother about whether your fellow Christians made progress in the Christian life or not. You would still be interested in 'number one', the Holy Spirit works in us to help us love one another.

Now don't get me wrong, I don't want to suggest that we are like empty jugs and that God is pouring all these things into us. We are responsible people and we are called upon to act responsibly and not to "quench the Spirit", (1 Thessalonians 5:19), nor to "grieve him" (Ephesians 4:30). When we stop meditating on what God has done for us in Christ, we may well feel as if we are not God's children. When we become careless with regard to temptation and loving God's people we may temporarily lose our assurance. But because the Spirit is at work in us we should quickly and consistently co-operate with Him and the result will be very reassuring.

All these aspects of the new life are objective ones and observable. The death of Jesus and our changed attitudes can be seen.

I have described in this chapter how to reassure ourselves when we feel as if we are not Christians. Thankfully we don't always or often feel like that.

Paul tells of another work of the Holy Spirit which is subjective and is also reassuring.

A reassuring experience

You will have known those times when the wonder of God's love is very real to you. In fact, it's so real that it's almost overwhelming. You have felt the wonder and relief that your sins have been forgiven and that you really are a child of God. Knowing God as Father is more real than anything else and you find words hard to describe your love for Him. It might be at a time of answered prayer or when you recalled what Jesus had done for you. Paul says that this is another evidence of the work of the Holy Spirit: ". . . by him [the Holy Spirit] we cry, 'Abba, Father.' The Spirit himself testifies with our spirit that we are God's children" (Romans 8:15b–16). 'Abba' is a term of greatest endearment.

God has spoken to reassure. He has acted in history in Christ's death and resurrection for us. He has acted by His Holy Spirit in us to reassure us.

You may be saying, "It sounds terrific but you don't know how weak and unreliable I am." Many people tell me the reason they baulk at becoming Christians is because they are frightened that they would never be able to keep going. I have much sympathy for them. Knowing myself I have to agree with them. Left to my own resources I wouldn't keep going either, but I'm not alone, I have the assurance of God's help.

3. God has promised

In addition to the other things which God has done to reassure us, He has made certain promises about our future. Jesus says in John 10:28,29 "I give them [His sheep] eternal life, and they shall never perish; no-one can snatch them out of my hand. My Father, who has given them to me is greater than all; no-one can snatch them out of my Father's hand". And in John 6:39 "This is the will of him who sent me, that I shall lose none of all that he has given me, but raise them up at the last day."

The writer to the Hebrews expresses the promise of God like this, "Therefore, he is able to save completely those who come to God through him, because he always lives to intercede for them" (Hebrews 7:25).

These promises have reassured me time and again. It is not so much a matter of how strong I am and my ability to hold on to God. It is a matter of how powerful He is and His ability to hold on to me. No one is more powerful than God, not even you yourself. No one will pluck them out of His hands. It is very reassuring, isn't it? Since it is the Father's will that Jesus should lose none of those whom God gives Him, we can be sure Jesus will do the will of His Father. He will bring us right through to the last day. He is well able to do this indefinitely because He never stops praying for us.

But I'm not perfect

One night after a Billy Graham Crusade I was chatting with a group of young people who had committed their lives to Jesus Christ during the Crusade. I said how good it was to know for certain that we were Christians.

One girl said, "I really find it hard to stop sinning?"

"I don't," I replied. "I find it impossible".

"Well, what will happen to us?"

"We have all been forgiven. The blood of Jesus cleanses us from all sin," I tried to reassure her.

"I thought that only meant all the ones up until I became a Christian".

"That would be good, but certainly not good enough," I explained. "There's no way we can be perfect except when we go to be with Jesus".

"Are you sure about that?" she asked. Together we looked at the great promises which God has made to us.

"What a relief that is," she said, "I've been so worried. I really wondered whether I was a Christian or not".

How I felt for her. I'd often stood where she stood. I knew how she felt. How I thank God that we can be sure.

I will be surprised if you have not felt like it too. The first time we sin after we have been converted can come as a big shock to us. You can be sure the devil will try and tell you that nothing really happened to change your life. It is then that Christians can become confused and wonder if they ought to pray again the prayer in chapter twelve.

Let me use the marriage illustration again. When two people marry they make absolute promises. They will love and cherish each other under all circumstances and what's more they will do so forever. As they start to live out those promises it will soon become apparent to them that they are easier to make than to keep. At best they never do more than approximate to them. At worst you would hardly know they had made them. Let us suppose we have a couple who have just had a fight. What do they do now? There need to be admissions, apologies and forgiveness. They will do all that because they do love each other and because they *have* made the promises they did. However, they don't need to get remarried. Even at the height of the argument, they are still married. There is the ring on the third finger. There is the marriage certificate. There are all the witnesses who heard the promises and there are (probably) the children. There is a lot of evidence that they are married. They do need to stop fighting if it's going to be any good, but they don't need to get remarried.

When we came to Christ our promises were far reaching and absolute. As we live out those promises the best we will do is approximate to them. When we fail we need to admit and apologise. God for His part will forgive. You don't, however, have to become a Christian again. There is God's word, there are God's actions and His promises. All are wonderful evidences to you that it did 'really take' for you.

Being a Christian is fundamentally different from marriage in one very important aspect. There is no dissolving of this relationship. It is forever, thank goodness.

CHAPTER FOURTEEN

Which Way is Forward?

When people get married they don't know *everything* about each other. They know enough to commit themselves in a binding relationship. As they live with each other they learn more and more about each other. The more they learn the better able they are to please each other (or otherwise). So the relationship is both developing and expanding. It is not static, it is either getting better or getting worse.

Most people before they are married are fairly independent and only have to please themselves. It is no small thing for a person who hasn't had to worry too much about anyone but 'number one' to be promising to "love and cherish in sickness and in health. . ." another. Now each is called upon to think first about the interests of another, to readjust a whole life style.

When we commit our lives to Jesus Christ as our Lord and Saviour the new life has many similarities. We said that we would set out to obey the Lord Jesus. But what does that mean in the life situation? What does Jesus really want us to do? To answer that we need to get to know Him.

After church one morning we were having a 'cuppa' and one of the ladies brought me a cup and said, "I'm sure you must be thirsty after having spoken for so long." (I wasn't sure if that was a hint about my preaching!)

"Thank you," I said. "Is it tea or coffee?"

"Tea."

"I generally drink coffee, but tea is O.K. Oh, there is milk in it. I generally drink it black, but I can drink it with milk," I said.

"I've put two sugars in it," she said.

"I really can't drink it with sugar".

You see I am a crass Australian. If I were an Oriental, I would have smiled and drunk it down and smiled again.

It's a small matter but do you see what was happening? That lady, in her kindness, had set out to please me and her feelings had taken action. She not only thought about acting kindly she really did it. However, because she really didn't know what *did* please me, the end result was less satisfactory than if she had.

It is essential that we get to know Jesus as soon as possible.

Up till now we have been at the centre of our own lives. We have made up the rules and said what is right and wrong for us. It is no small adjustment to make to start to have another take first place. Christ is to take first place from now on.

Many years ago I was invited to attend a small gathering of men who met together for about an hour a week to encourage each other in living the Christian life. One man admitted, "I know that in any given situation I should behave exactly like the Lord Jesus. My real difficulty is that in most of the situations in which I find myself I honestly don't know how Jesus would behave." I thought his statement was profound. That was more than twenty-five years ago, and I wonder if he would say now, "My real problem is that when I do know what Jesus would do, I really do find it difficult to do it His way." It certainly is what I would say.

There are several ways in which we can be helped to get to know Jesus better and to obey Him.

1. READING THE BIBLE

Now that you have become a Christian, the regular reading of the Bible must become a part of your life.

What makes the Bible so important?

a) *It is all about Jesus.* Jesus is at the centre of all God's plans. In the Gospel of Matthew again and again, the writer says that Jesus said and did things to "fulfil the scriptures". These scriptures were the Old Testament. They pointed to Jesus as they looked forward to the coming King who would rescue and protect the people of God. The New Testament is all about the fulfilment of the Old Testament in Jesus, together with what that means in the way people are to live in fellowship with Him.

The Bible is where we get information about Him so that we will know how to please Him.

Sometimes when you read the Bible this will be crystal clear. When you read the Gospels or the New Testament letters you will see that they focus directly on the Lord Jesus. Sometimes it is not always so easy to recognise Jesus. It is much more subtle. The Old Testament deals with God calling a people, the Jews, to serve Him. Yet this nation was a preparation for the coming of Jesus and He is the fulfilment of all God's promises to them. He is the central theme of the book, so when I go to the Bible, I'm looking to find Jesus. I ask it, "What are you telling me about Jesus?" The tragedy is that some people have the book and read it but still do not recognise Jesus. Reading the book is not an end in itself. It is the means of getting to know Jesus. Yet even knowing about Jesus is not an end in itself. It is a means to our being able to obey Jesus and live as God wants us to.

b) *It is the word of God.* Christians believe the Bible is the word of God because Jesus believed that it was so. Many Christians have discovered that when they read the Bible now, it really is quite different from what it was before they became Christians. You will hear God speaking through its pages not as an audible voice, but as you discover and learn what is written about Him. Before I became a Christian I didn't find the Bible very interesting. I didn't understand it nor did I enjoy it. When I became a Christian, it seemed to leap to life. It was where I found God. I didn't always understand it but I understood much more than I had before. What was happening was that God's Holy Spirit now lived in my life and He was teaching me from the Bible as I read it.

Your experience may not be the same as mine. But you too will 'meet' God in the pages of the Bible and as you get to know Him more and more your friendship will develop.

Many people in our time do not believe the Bible is the word of God. Some reject it all. Others want to reject parts of it. So it will probably be valuable to spend some time looking at Jesus' attitude towards the Bible. To have Jesus as our Lord means that we believe what He believes.

For Jesus, the scriptures [Old Testament] were God's word. God spoke through them (Matthew 19:4,5). They were binding and must be fulfilled. Jesus said, "Everything must be fulfilled that is written about me in the Law of Moses, the Prophets and the Psalms" (Luke 24:44). The scriptures cannot be broken (John 10:35). There is a recurring phrase which the Gospel writers use, [He did] ". . . this to fulfil the scriptures" (John 13:18; 19:36).

Jesus was able to resist the temptations of the devil by His understanding of and obedience to the scriptures. Each time He was tempted, Jesus said "It is written" (Matthew 4:4,7,10). For Jesus what the Bible said, was what God said (Luke 4:4).

When Jesus referred to the scriptures He was referring to the Old Testament. The New Testament was not written until after Jesus had gone back to heaven.

At the Last Supper, Jesus promised that He would send the Holy Spirit to the apostles in such a way that:

i) they would remember everything which Jesus had told them (John 14:26)

ii)   they would be led into all truth (John 16:13)
iii)   they would be taught by Him (John 14:26)

We can be sure that Jesus has kept this promise and that the New Testament is as factually the word of God, as is the Old Testament.

c) It will help us to be godly. Following the example of their Lord, the apostles believe the Bible to be the word of God. Here is a classic statement of St. Paul: "All Scripture is God-breathed and is useful for teaching, rebuking, correcting and training in righteousness, so that the man of God may be thoroughly equipped for every good work" (2 Timothy 3:16,17).

What can the Bible do for us? Paul says it will *teach* us about God and about how we can live the Christian life. It gives us all the information we need to grow like Jesus. Along the road of life it is the map showing us which way to go. However, if we stray off that road through carelessness or ignorance, it will *rebuke* us. We won't be left driving around in some paddock. We will discover that something is wrong by its words. It we continue to read it, it will *correct* us. It will show us the way back on to the roadway. This book *trains* us in righteousness. What could be more valuable? No wonder it has been a world bestseller if it will do all that. Paul concludes this summary by saying that the Bible will *equip* us for everything which is godly so that if we obey it, we will know how to do every good work.

It does this because it is the word of God.

As we read this book, our minds are informed so that we can take action in a godly way.

You can see how important the reading of the Bible is. You can be sure that the devil will do everything in his power to stop you from doing it. He has no desire at all to see you grow up into a godly person. His aim for you will be to hold you back and frustrate your growth. Don't give him any pleasure in this regard.

How to use it

When it comes to using the Bible there are some things we should bear in mind. We need to study it:

a) Seriously

God took care to bring the Bible to us and it contains exactly what He wanted to say. Its authors came from a diverse background, and are separated in time by hundreds of years yet its theme is the same. The Holy Spirit was assisting them so that God's word would come to us today. Since God did this for us we should take care to read it carefully. What the Bible says is what God says. It is not a magic book but an inspired book. It means what it says, we should take it seriously.

God says, "This is the one I esteem: he who is humble and contrite in spirit and trembles at my word" (Isaiah 66:2).

b) Obediently

The apostle James says, "Do not merely listen to the word, and so deceive yourselves. Do what it says" (James 1:22).

Since it is the word of God, we should come to the Bible with a spirit of humility and obedience, looking to the Holy Spirit to teach us its true meaning. It is a book which will only ever be understood by those who will obey it. Jesus said, "If any one chooses to do God's will, he will find out whether my teaching comes from God or whether I speak on my own" (John 7:17). This is an interesting comment. Only those who desire to obey God will recognise that Jesus' teaching comes from God. This is a constant principle of the Christian life. Those who will obey will discover more. Those who won't, know less and less.

You will see that being a Christian has nothing to do with being clever (otherwise there would be few Christians). Yet, being bright is not a barrier unless it gives people an inflated idea of their own worth in the Christian life, then it is a menace. Being ordinary is no barrier to real understanding of the Bible's message.

This was shown to me one evening at a dinner for church members. I got into talking to a young man who was I suspect what is termed "a slow learner", he asked me, "What part of the Bible have you been studying lately?"

I replied that I had just finished working through the letter to the Hebrews.

"That seems a bit too hard for me. Do you understand it?" he asked. I told him that I was a little uncertain about some of it, but that generally speaking I thought that I did understand it, and I asked him what he had been reading.

"I'm studying the letter to the Romans," he said.

"Do you understand it?" I asked. I don't think it is the easiest part of the Bible myself and was interested in his comment.

"Not all of it. But I read it over and over again and each time I understand more than I did before. I'm going to keep reading it until I really know what it means."

I think he probably will too.

c) To find Jesus

I have already made the point that the Bible is all about Jesus. So we study it to find Him.

On one occasion Jesus said to a group of religious people, "You diligently study the Scriptures because you think that by them you possess eternal life. These are the Scriptures which testify about me, yet you refuse to come to me to have life" (John 5:39,40). What a tragedy! They thought that the act of reading the Bible would gain them eternal life. They read it and missed its point completely. They didn't know it was all about Jesus.

The first question to be asked when I read the Bible is, "What does it tell me about Jesus?" When that has been answered, then the next question is, "What must I do to please Him?" We need to *do* something as a result of reading it.

Don't worry if you don't always understand it. Make a note of difficult parts and ask some Christian to help you. Another person will be able to understand some parts better than you do and vice versa. Don't be frightened to admit you don't understand. It's easier to get clarification when we don't pretend.

When you find really marvellous things in the Bible it's worth making a note of them so that you can share them with other people. It will be a help to them and it will also help to impress it more clearly on you too.

Where to begin

When you start reading most books it's no problem to know where to begin. You begin at chapter one — at the beginning.

The Bible is not quite like that because it is really a collection of books bound together.

My advice to the beginner would be to start by reading from the New Testament, a Gospel, either Matthew, Mark, Luke or John. In those we find the sayings and actions of Jesus described as clearly as anywhere. When you have finished those, you could then read the Acts of the Apostles, a book which tells us the history of the early Christians. From there I think I would recommend from the Old Testament, Genesis and Exodus which tell about the beginning of the world, of man's rebelling, and of God's plan for His people. After that, back to the New Testament, the Epistle to the Romans.

I suggest you talk with your Christian friends about the Bible reading programme they follow. The Bible Society and the Scripture Union have Bible reading programmes and notes to help us. Some churches have their own.

It has been my habit for many years to read some part of the Bible every day rather than just whenever I feel like it (or remember to). Sometimes I read a few chapters and at other times just a few verses. I normally do that first thing in the morning. I would encourage you to find a time and place each day when you can settle down and read it. It you don't have a Bible then the sooner you buy one the better. Get a modern translation. There are plenty of good ones available. I have quoted from a translation called *The New International Version* which I find very satisfactory. I have also found it helpful to keep a notebook handy in which I jot down the answers to my two questions. When I find a really helpful verse I often underline it so that when I am looking for it later, it is easy to find and I try to memorise some verses which seem to me very important.

However, in time you will be able to find the most satisfactory time, place and method which works for you. But whatever happens, get with it as soon as possible.

2. PRAYING

If the Bible is the way God speaks to us then the way we speak to Him is through prayer. It is the most natural way for us to cultivate our new friendship with God and nothing reminds me more about it than does prayer.

It would be a very strange relationship indeed if we didn't speak to God. Before I became a Christian I sometimes said set prayers, but it had never occurred to me that God could be approached as a real friend. I used to think that God was probably fairly busy and didn't want to be interrupted. Nothing is further from the truth. God's complaint with Israel was that, although He had done so much for them, "Yet you have not called upon me, O Jacob" (Isaiah 43:22).

The apostle Paul tells the Thessalonians to "pray continually" (1 Thessalonians 5:17).

The example of Jesus

Not only is Jesus God the Son, but He is also the perfect person and as such is our model for life. The Bible writers show us Jesus often at prayer. At moments of great trial (Matthew 11:25; 26:39), and at times when life was busy and He was snowed under, He withdrew to a quiet spot for prayer (Luke 4:42; Matthew 14:23; Mark 1:35).

It was His own example in prayer which caused the disciples to ask Him to teach them to pray. He did so with the Lord's Prayer (Luke 11:1-4); He followed it up with two parables about prayer (Luke 11:5-7 and 11:11-13), and this word of encouragement, "Ask and it will be given to you; seek and you will find; knock and the door will be opened to you (Luke 11:9). He prayed for His disciples (Luke 22:32; John 17:9). He prayed at times of great rejoicing (Mark 6:39-46) and when important decisions were to be made (Luke 6:12-13). He prayed at moments when great works were being performed (John 11:41). It was the regular pattern of His life.

How to pray

Any time is a good time to pray. Often during the day I find that I am engaged in activities which don't really require much thought. I often speak with God at those times (although I've given up closing my eyes, particularly while driving the car!) and just as I would with any friend, I share good times and bad. I tell Him of my hopes and aspirations, of my fears and my problems. Because He is who He is I often ask for benefits to be given to my friends and to the nations of the world.

The more I read the Bible the more I am encouraged to ask 'big'. I used to think that it really wasn't good form to be always asking for things in prayer, but then I realised that every part of the Lord's Prayer was an asking (Luke 11:1-4), and I have come to see that the more I ask the more I honour God. When I am praying for peace in Northern Ireland (which I often do), I am saying, "O God, I believe you are in charge of history and can work in the lives of men and bring peace out of chaos." Even a simple prayer for rain honours God, because its basis is that God can do it because He is Lord of the world. If I forgot to thank God for my food, in time I would forget that God is its giver and I would start to take it all for granted.

Do you always get an answer?

I met a man who told me that he had given up prayer because he never got the things he asked for. There could only be one reason for that. He must have always asked for the wrong things.

There is no doubt that God always hears the prayers of His people and He *always* answers them. However, that is not to say we will always get what we ask for.

God's answer will be directed toward our good. That is what He has promised in His commitment to us. Sometimes we think we know what is best and we are mistaken. No one muscles God around. He can't be manipulated and what's more He never needs to be. He has our best interests at heart all the time.

Like any responsible father, God answers our prayer in one of three ways. He may say, "Yes", "No" or "Not yet". All of my prayers have been answered in one of those ways. I say this because often when I hear Christians speak, they give the impression that God always says, "Yes". This is not the case. If we ask God to do what we know is against His declared will, we can be certain the answer is "No". So when you know what the answer is already, it is childish to persist in asking.

When I say God answers our prayers, I don't want to give the impression that you will hear a voice speaking to you. In spite of the fact that some people claim to have heard a 'voice', it has never been my experience. The Bible does not suggest it will happen. God normally answers our prayers through the circumstances of life or through our increased knowledge of Him. Since He has the world at His disposal, He will answer you in a way which you will recognise and understand.

There is only one thing for which there would be no answer at all, and that is when we ask God to do something which is against His will. When you know the answer already, don't fool around by asking.

Set times and places

As well as praying at various times during the day I have found it helpful to have a set time when I pray. A good time is after I have read my Bible, and I usually follow a pattern. I begin by thanking God for who He is and what He has done for me. I then get anything which is worrying me off my chest, especially if I've done the wrong thing. Then I pray for other people, including members of my family and those who are engaged in the spread of the Gospel. Finally I pray for myself (someone I never forget! Would you believe it?)

I try to keep a list of my requests so that when God gives me an answer, I won't forget to thank Him.

Pray alone and with others

Not only do I pray by myself, but I find it helpful from time to time to pray with others. You could pray about matters of mutual interest. You may have some Christian friends who will be glad to do this with you, or you may be in a position where you can pray as a family.

3.   MEETING WITH THE CHURCH

When God created mankind His stated aim was that we should be "in his image" and "have dominion over the creation" (Genesis 1:26). His purpose was that He would have a people who would live together reflecting both individually and corporately His character; people who would rule the world under His authority.

As we have seen, that was interrupted temporarily by mankind turning away from God. He, through Jesus, calls back to Himself a people who will live for "the praise of his glory" (Ephesians 1:12). We come into fellowship with God individually but we immediately become members of God's family, the church. Each of us is born individually but we will not survive unless we are looked after. We cannot sustain ourselves.

The Bible knows nothing of a 'lone-ranger' type Christian. Christianity is personal, but *not* private. For a person to say, "I am Christ's man but I never meet with the church", is a complete contradiction in terms. Such a person doesn't understand God's plan to call together people, not just individuals.

When we meet with God's people it will obviously help us to grow stronger as Christians. I have used the word 'church' to mean the Christians when they meet. Don't ever confuse the building with the church. The building is really a rain shelter to protect the Christians when they meet as the church.

When you became a Christian, you not only became a friend of God but you became a member of God's family, and like your own family, you have no choice about your brothers and sisters, and so it is in the family of God — the church.

If I had been put in charge of picking the members of the church I attend, I would not have picked all of them, and I am sure that they certainly wouldn't have picked me! However, the more I meet with them and see what God is doing in them and with them, the more I have grown to appreciate them and to marvel at how really great God is. Let me tell you about them and why I like meeting with them.

First of all there's my minister. His main job is to teach us the Bible and to call on us to obey it. It's obvious to me that he really works hard at this and I think I'm fortunate to have him. He isn't the only one who teaches. Some of the others do that. They make a contribution in this area and bring to us their knowledge both from life and the Bible. In our church are some people with real problems and they are an inspiration to me in the way they battle on and look to Jesus for help. Just knowing them helps me to live the Christian life.

Some of the members are new Christians just like you are and their joining us was as exciting as every new arrival is in a family. I don't know if you feel threatened by church. I think all 'babies' do. If the people at your church are like ours they will be overjoyed to meet you.

In our church are people with some real talent. Some of them play musical instruments; some make things; some teach children at school; some run activities for the rest of us. As families go, we are fairly large. As churches go, we are fairly average. There is a good cross section — some old, some middle-aged and some young. Some have been Christians for a very long time and it's great to know them.

What I like best about our church family is that they really are trying to grow like Jesus and they encourage me to do the same. Often they tell me they have been praying for me and this has been helpful too. Like all families we don't always agree and when that happens we need to take steps to correct our mistakes. When we meet as the church our meeting is fairly formal, but we also meet in smaller less formal groups. It helps me to be with them. I realise I'm not alone.

Everyone a minister

The Bible says that all Christians have gifts to be used in the life of the family and that as we meet both formally and informally, we are to help each other grow like Christ (see Ephesians 4:11-14). We are to minister to each other. To minister is to serve each other. Often the persons who are paid by the church to do that all the time, are called ministers, but strictly speaking, we should all be serving each other. Sometimes the Bible gives names to our gifts from God, but I don't think you need to worry too much about them at this stage. What we all need to know is that all the gifts are to be directed to the same end. That we will all grow like Jesus. I've found it more helpful to ask, "What can I do to help these people now to grow like Christ?" rather than "I wonder what my gift really is?" If I ask the first question, you can be sure that I will start to use my gifts even if I don't know what to call them.

However, don't fall into the trap of thinking you will

have no contribution to make. Church is not like a concert where some perform and others are spectators. When we meet we are all to share ourselves and our gifts with the others.

A word of warning

Don't put any of the church people on a pedestal or have romantic ideas about what they will be like. They are ordinary people like us. I saw on the back of a car a small sticker which said, "Christians aren't perfect, just forgiven". That is very true. We are all working at growing like Jesus, and some have made more or less progress than others.

Some at church may not really be Christians yet. Not really in the family. So don't let them confuse you. Some people have told me of bad experiences they have had in the churches they've attended. I'm sorry about that. It hasn't been my experience, and by and large I'm impressed with the way they help me to be Christian.

Which one?

If you haven't been in the habit of going to church and you are about to make a choice, you may appreciate some help. My problem is that I'm biased. I think the church I attend is the best!

If you have Christian friends, you may want to go with them. However, if not, look for one where the teachers believe the Bible is the word of God and carefully teach it. Unfortunately I cannot say this of all churches so find out before you settle. If you are in doubt, ask them. If the Bible is not believed and taught properly, there is no way the members will know how to exercise their gifts. Ask God to help you as you make a decision, but I do urge you to resist the temptation to stay at home. None of us is self-sufficient, we need others and they need us.

Church at work
You may find that where you work the Christians meet together to encourage each other. In most schools where I taught, we had a Christian fellowship of teachers and children who met over lunch one day a week. You'll probably find details of similar meetings on the notice board which you've passed a hundred times and never noticed. It's bound to tell you when and where they meet.

4. SHARING CHRIST WITH OTHERS
Sharing Christ and your new life as a Christian with others is a great privilege as well as a responsibility. There is no doubt that God wants others to know about Jesus, and both love for God and love for our fellow man will make us want to tell them. Some people find it harder to do than others. In the days which follow your new life, no doubt your friends and relatives will notice the change and ask you why. You will get a good chance to tell them about what Jesus has done for you and for them too. I cannot guarantee their reactions, but I guess they will react like you did when you first heard!

As soon as you can, you should teach yourself the gospel (the good news) so that you can explain it. I have written a book for Christians to help them to do that. It is called *Know and Tell the Gospel* (Hodder). However don't wait until you've read it, start now. You may find the story in John 9:1-41 helpful. That man didn't know a great deal but he did know something, "One thing I do know. I was blind but now I see" he said to his friends.

Start praying that you will get a chance to tell your friends about Jesus, and that God will show you when that time has come.

Don't get discouraged
Five year old Michael went to school for the first time. He was delighted at the prospect of school and wild with

excitement when at last the day arrived. He was glad to be taken and glad to be left there. When his father collected him at 3 pm he asked Michael, "How did you get on?" Dad was slightly shaken by the answer.

"It was hopeless."

"Whatever happened?" said the worried father.

"I've been at that school all day and I *still* can't read or write," was the frustrated reply.

In the Christian life there is no way you'll be 'reading and writing' after the first day. These days Michael really doesn't have any trouble reading or writing, but he is halfway through High School now. It will be like that for you. You won't become godly at once and that may be frustrating in the beginning. Over a period of time you will make steady progress if you work in the areas I've suggested, Bible reading, prayer and fellowship with other Christians.

When we committed our lives to Christ He enrolled us as disciples. None of us ever stops being a learner. We spend a life time learning to be good disciples. You can become a Christian in a moment, but you spend a life time learning to live the Christian life.

It's very like marriage, at its best. You say, "I will." It only takes a moment in time; you spend the rest of your life learning to live out the implications of that promise.

I find the Christian life fairly hard to live, but very, very satisfying.

Have a great time!

P.S. . . .

I want to end this book on a positive note. Christians are often criticised for being so heavenly minded that they are of no earthly use. I don't want to be like that. I live in a world where there is much poverty, sickness and unhappiness, where powerless people cannot resist the unjust forces around them. I live in a world where there is much unbelief in the living God. I don't want to be a useless, religious no-hoper.

We have responsibilities and obligations in this world. We are to "do good to all people, especially to those who belong to the family of believers" (Galatians 6:10). Everyone's greatest need is to come to Christ. Of that there is no doubt. It is not however their only need, and we do less than justice to God's word if we pretend that it is.

God is concerned about every aspect of our lives. He is interested in marriage, family life, work, church and society in general. In fact, it was God who ordained them. He hasn't left us in the dark about how He wants us to behave in every aspect of life. Let me describe a Christian couple to show what I mean.

John and Mary have been married for ten years. They have two children. Both of John's parents are dead and so is Mary's mother. John is a salesman, and in addition to looking after the family, Mary has a part time job at the local supermarket. They committed their lives to Christ several years ago. The Bible has clear teaching on how as husband and wife they should treat each other.

As parents the Bible instructs them about the way they should relate to their children. But they are not living an insulated, isolated life. They are both citizens of Australia and members of their church. They are both employees. They both belong to a local tennis club and the Parents Association of the local school. They have responsibility for Mary's father. The way John and Mary live in all the various aspects of their life is of importance and concern to God. Their entire lives are to come under the control of Jesus. The Bible has guidelines for them in all the different areas of their existence in this world.

When we become Christians most of us have little knowledge of what God expects from us. Some aspects of life are relatively easy, for example being a good citizen; others will be quite difficult, for example being an enthusiastic employee if I have a boring job. We are not automatically or instantly transformed into people who behave as mature Christians.

God accepts us completely because of Christ and not because we are good, and it is because we have been accepted and forgiven that we will want to learn God's will for every situation of life. Then when we know what pleases Him we can work away with His help at becoming better at it. Our lives should be marked by goodness, especially in relationships with other people.

You will see what I mean by referring to the following passages in the Bible: Romans chapters 12 and 13; Colossians chapter 3; 1 Peter 2:11 to 3:7.

On the other hand it is possible to be so earthly minded that we are of no heavenly use. That would be equally unbalanced.

Let me finish by saying the best is yet to come. Whatever the future has in store for you you can be certain that God will guide you through life right to the end.

"We know that in all things God works for the good of those who love him, who have been called according to his purpose. For those God foreknew he also predestined to be conformed to the likeness of his Son, that he might be the first born among many brothers.

And those he predestined he also called; those he
called, he also justified; those he justified, he also glorified" (Romans 8:28–30).

When you turned to Christ you may not have fully
realised the truth of what Paul is saying. We turned to
Christ because God chose us to be His people whom He
calls out to grow like Christ. He called us back. He justified us and He is working all things for our good now
and He will glorify us when He makes us perfect in the
day when Jesus returns.

This great purpose of God for us should fill us with
wonder and awe. It should cause us to bend every effort
of our will to that end.

Cricket is amongst the most popular of all international
sports today, and it is a great honour to be chosen to play
for one's country. Only eleven in all the thousands who
play the game are chosen to play in a Test Match. Imagine
you are one who is lucky enough to do that, and that I
am the manager of the team. When we get to the last
day of the match I realise that there are only ten men
fielding. "Where is Tom Smith?"

"I think he went fishing," is the reply. I rush off to
find him.

"What are you doing here? Get changed and get on
the field. There are hundreds of cricketers in this country who would give their eye teeth to take your place.
You weren't selected to fish, you were chosen to play
cricket. So get on!"

It is an unbelievable privilege to have been selected to
be in God's team. His team is one where we are demon-
strating to the whole creation how marvellous God is
(Ephesians 3:10,11), and we are meant to grow into
Christ-likeness (Romans 8:29). Make sure you are "on
the field" and not "fishing".

Make sure the way you practise shows how seriously
you take the 'game' and what a real privilege it is to be
chosen.

Whether the 'game' is long or short there is no doubt about who will win:

"Listen, I tell you a mystery: We will not all sleep, but we will all be changed — in a flash, in the twinkling of an eye, at the last trumpet. For the trumpet will sound, the dead will be raised imperishable, and we will be changed. *But thanks be to God! He gives us the victory through our Lord Jesus Christ.* Therefore, my dear brothers, stand firm. Let nothing move you. Always give yourselves fully to the work of the Lord, because you know that your labour in the Lord is not in vain" (1 Corinthians 15:51,57,58).

Michael Green

WHY BOTHER WITH JESUS?

'Why bother?' considers Michael Green, is a widespread disease. Nothing seems to matter any more so long as we have our increase in wages and the cost of our comforts is not too high. The disease has taken hold of our concern for the truth. When matters of right and wrong are settled by head-count rather than principle, a moral collapse could well be in the offing.

From this grim diagnosis Michael Green asks 'Why Bother With Jesus?', looking in detail at the qualities in Jesus which make us want to learn more about him.

John Chapman

KNOW AND TELL THE GOSPEL

Many Christians don't know how to begin to tell others about their faith. Yet evangelism is central to Christianity. *Know and Tell the Gospel* clearly explains the biblical basis for evangelism and how to communicate faith naturally but powerfully.

'Being engaged in evangelism is exciting, rewarding, the privilege and responsibility of every Christian,' affirms the author. With a foreword by Gavin Reid and Eddie Gibbs.

Michael Green

NEW LIFE, NEW LIFESTYLE

A new life means a new lifestyle and the Christian life is an exciting adventure, a whole new world of experience. Michael Green points the way forward for the new believer.

'Having found Christ, we want to explore him more and more, and give ourselves over to him in every department of our lives. That is the very heart of the Christian life: getting to know him better, and working out the implications of it in our behaviour and attitudes, our career and relationships.'

David Watson

IS ANYONE THERE?

How can we find God? David Watson emphasises the relevance and urgency of this question for today, and sets out clearly the facts about Jesus, and how he is the way to God.

'One half of us finds it difficult to believe in God, but the other half is intrigued by the possibility that he really might exist. There is this unquestionable search for some kind of spiritual reality that will lift us out of ourselves to what is real and true . . . without God, life is extraordinarily bleak.'